Dearest Ge_____

Many thank_ _____ _____
with this boo_ _____ ____ed.
May gods' word light" up
your life. 'Αγαπη
*Χρ_*

The Nine Pillars of
Spirituality

The gifts of the Holy Spirit

Christos Demetriou

ACTS International Limited, West Sussex, England

Dedicated to the blessed Holy Spirit.
Thank you for being my source of inspiration.
Not just for this book but for everything in life.

To my dearest wife, Loraine, and my daughter, Xana.
The two bright stars in my universe.

Thank you for being with me along every path, upon every mountain top and in every valley. It's been an exciting journey and I couldn't have done it without you.

Christos Demetriou is the founder and Senior Pastor of Cornerstone the Church, a vibrant multicultural community with members from 40 different nations based in Surrey, United Kingdom. Born in Cyprus, his fluent understanding of the Greek language enables him to convey unique insight into the New Testament scriptures. In this, his third book, it is his understanding of the original Greek text that enabled the unlocking and expounding of these profound Biblical principles and concepts.

Christos began his career in the music industry aged 17 where he was a successful songwriter and record producer, associated with over 160 recordings and a number of top five hits. Having worked (in different capacities) with artists such as Cat Stevens, David Bowie and Mike d'Abo, one of his songs was used during the opening ceremony of the London 2012 Olympic Games and appears in the Guinness Book of Records as the first time a 'sample' was used on a music track. Pastor Chris is also a notable media entrepreneur, his LinkedIn profile being one of the top 1% of the most viewed contacts globally. He presently lives in West Sussex with his wife, Loraine, and daughter, Xana.

ACTS International Limited, West Sussex, England

Text copyright © 2018 by Christos Demetriou
This edition copyright © 2018 ACTS International Ltd

Published by ACTS International Limited
West Sussex, England

ISBN   978-0-9557280-1-3   (Print)

ISBN   978-0-9557280-2-0   (e-Pub)

ISBN   978-0-9557280-3-7   (Kindle)

First Edition 2018

Acknowledgements
Unless otherwise stated, scripture quotations taken from the Holy Bible, New King James Version, copyright © 1979, 1980, 1982 by Thomas Nelson Inc. Used by permission of Thomas Nelson Inc. The "NKJ" and "New King James Version" trademarks are registered in the United States Patent and Trademark Office by Thomas Nelson Inc.

A catalogue record for this book is available from the British Library

Printed and bound in the UK, March 2018

Table of Contents

A Pillar of Fire was one of the manifestations of the presence of the God of Israel in the Torah.

1

What is Spirituality?

In modern society, spirituality is a broad concept with room for many perspectives, and it has many meanings. Spirituality may include a sense of connection to something bigger than ourselves (a greater power), and it typically involves a search for meaning to life. Some people describe a spiritual experience as sacred or transcendent or simply a deep sense of interconnectedness. In various world religions, a spiritual person presupposes that the human race is all "one," and therefore, each individual must consciously attempt to honour this "oneness" at all times. To others, being spiritual is synonymous with becoming a person whose highest priority is to be loving to oneself and others, someone who genuinely cares about people, animals and the planet.

Mystical spirituality maintains that all rivers lead to the same ocean, so there is no single true religion or faith. Consequently, when disagreement arises, this religious form of intellectualism attempts to bring about false unity. Other, similar 'mental assent' groups claim that spirituality encourages people to achieve a 'God consciousness' and instructs them on how to seek their own experiences through inner exploration and discovery.

Transcendentalism is founded on the idea that men and women, equally, have knowledge about themselves and the world around them that "transcends" or goes beyond what they can see, hear, taste, touch or feel. Also, Eco-Spirituality is thought to be a manifestation of the spiritual connection between human beings and the environment they live in. It is found in many forms of primal religions and is highlighted in a philosophical way in various practices of Buddhism (e.g. Chinese Hua-Yen Buddhism). Note, all of the above are fully accepted and integrated into today's politically correct society. Yet, none of them can claim to be truly spiritual.

The English dictionary defines spirituality as, 'the quality of being concerned with the human spirit or soul as opposed to material or physical things'. However, to a Christian, spirituality involves a personal choice. A choice to grow in a daily and lasting relationship with the Lord Jesus Christ by submitting to the ministry of the Holy Spirit. Jesus promised that the Holy Spirit would lead His followers "into all truth" (John 16:13). Part of that truth is taking the things of God and correctly applying them to everyday life. When that application is made, the believer then makes a choice to allow the Holy Spirit to control him/her. Genuine Christian spirituality is based upon the extent to which a born-again believer allows the God's Spirit to lead and control his or her life. Therefore, it is impossible for a Christian to be truly spiritual without the ongoing involvement of the Holy Spirit.

The apostle Paul stated that believers should be "filled" with the Holy Spirit. "Do not get drunk on wine, which leads to dissipation. Instead, be filled with the Spirit" (Ephesians 5:18). This passage is written in the imperative and continual tense, and therefore, it means "keep on being filled with the Spirit" or "be continually filled with the Spirit."

Being persistently filled with the Spirit is simply allowing God's Spirit to take complete control. Notice how authentic Christian spirituality is produced by the Spirit of God working in and through the believer on a frequent and continuous basis.

Furthermore, if the Spirit is constantly at work 'in and through' a Christian, then His gifts will be essential to sustaining spiritual growth and aiding spiritual development. God has always intended for His children to grow into maturity and fulfil their purpose. In Philippians 2:13 (Amplified) it says, "For it is [not your strength, but it is] God who is effectively at work in you, both to will and to work [that is, strengthening, energizing, and creating in you the longing and the ability to fulfil your purpose] for His good pleasure." God empowers both our "doing" (ἐνέργεια) and the "willing" that lies behind the "doing." So Christian spirituality has nothing to do with rules that regulate human conduct. Instead, it begins with a mind that is being transformed by the Spirit of God so as not to be conformed to this world but to the character of God Himself. That involves knowing God's will - what is good, pleasing and perfect to Him.

Christian spirituality is simply becoming more and more like Jesus Christ — being transformed into His image! Christlikeness is not produced by imitation but by inhabitation. Believers allow Christ to live through them (by His Spirit). "To them God willed to make known what are the riches of the glory of this mystery among the Gentiles: which is Christ in you, the hope of glory." (Colossians 1:27). How does this happen in real life? It happens through the choices people make. Christians must choose to do the right thing in situations they are confronted with, and then trust God's Spirit to equip them with His power and the wisdom to do His will. Since the Holy Spirit lives inside, they are able to do exactly what Jesus would do if He were present. This is an important function of God's Spirit here on earth!

When Jesus ascended and sat down at the right hand of God, He made sure that His followers were not left as orphans (John 14:18). He sent the Holy Spirit to act as their guide and Helper. The Greek word used in John 14:16 παράχλητος ("another helper") implies that the Spirit is the One who draws alongside to help believers do exactly what Jesus would do if He was present. Earlier, in John 14:12, Jesus declared, "Most assuredly, I say to you, he who believes in Me, the works that I do he will do also; and greater works than these he will do, because I go to My Father."

Therefore, another measure of Christian spirituality must be the ability for a follower of Christ to do the things Jesus did and this is where spirituality becomes a serious matter. Christians now have the power to affect every area of life, through the Spirit that is at work in them. What's more, the Holy Spirit working "in and through" a believer will always include a manifestation of His gifts. For without the Gifts of the Holy Spirit in operation, no one would be able to do what Jesus did, and no one would be able to enforce the victory (secured in Christ according to the mighty power and authority He gave to the church).

What is the exceeding greatness of His power toward us who believe, according to the working of His mighty power which He worked in Christ when He raised Him from the dead and seated Him at His right hand in the heavenly places, far above all principality and power and might and dominion, and every name that is named, not only in this age but also in that which is to come. And He put all things under His feet, and gave Him to be head over all things to the church, which is His body, the fullness of Him who fills all in all. (Ephesians 1:19-23)

The mightiest power ever unleashed on this earth was not the power of atomic bombs; it was not the power of an earthquake, volcano, tornado, hurricane, or flood. The mightiest power ever unleashed on this earth was when God raised Jesus Christ from the dead. If the forces of evil could have kept Jesus from being resurrected from the dead, they would have been triumphant. Hence, in this passage, the apostle Paul uses "forceful" words to make the point that God's power in raising Jesus from the dead was the mightiest display of power ever witnessed.

The four different words used here, "rule, authority, power, and dominion," encompass all spiritual powers. Therefore, whatever levels of spiritual power and authority that exist, Jesus is greater than them all. Paul adds, "not only in this age but also in the one to come" to make it clear that Jesus Christ is exalted to the place of absolute, supreme and unlimited power in the entire universe. Besides, His authority is not just for a period of time but for all eternity.

Yet, what has this to do with true Christian spirituality? Well, if spirituality can be measured according to what the Holy Spirit is doing 'in and through' believers, it is important to grasp and acknowledge that the exceeding greatness of God's power is already at work.

Here are two things that must be understood and then fully embraced: (1) This exceedingly great and mighty power is available to the Church right now, and (2), it is at work in the Church exclusively to glorify Jesus. That is why the Gifts of the Holy Spirit are so important. The Spirit has a clear mandate, and that is, to bring glory to Jesus Christ. Just as Jesus had a clear directive to bring glory to His Father (John 17:1-3), and the only way this can be effectively executed is for the Body of Christ to do the very things that Jesus did ("and even greater things than these").

This suggests that the main "pillars" of the Church are the nine Gifts of the Holy Spirit. For, without them in operation, the power and authority the apostle Paul was talking about could never be realised or experienced. More importantly, all spiritual powers would not have to surrender to the authority Jesus passed on to His Church. These nine pillars represent strength and stability, and they sustain a believer as he or she matures to a place whereby they can be used to extend God's kingdom here on earth. A pillar is often something that is considered a support or foundation. However, these nine pillars are the cornerstones of what sits at the heart of Christian spirituality. Each pillar is of equal importance. In fact, they are often referred to as the instruments that effectively build or edify the Church. Spiritual gifts are empowerments for edifying the church and extending the Kingdom of God.

In 1 Corinthians 14, as the apostle Paul instructs the church at Corinth on the function of spiritual gifts, he repeats several times that they are to strengthen or build up the church. Implying that without these "pillars", the church would be weak, unstable and ineffective. I am fully persuaded that the nine Gifts of the Holy Spirit are an absolute necessity. Believers are expected to mature spiritually to a place where the power of God is present in greater measure than before. A place that is visible to both believer and unbeliever alike.

Yet, this cannot happen unless the Holy Spirit is operating His gifts in the Church today.

So, what exactly are these gifts? Spiritual gifts are supernatural empowerments given by the Holy Spirit to the followers of Christ so that they can do the work of building up the Body of Christ, that is the Church, and extend the Kingdom of God throughout the world.

Spiritual gifts are not intuitive, inherent, natural talents, like an ear for music or the ability to paint or draw, rather they are empowerments that the Holy Spirit gives to a believer to act in ways that were not possible by mere natural effort apart from the Holy Spirit. In the ministry of the apostles (the Book of Acts), we see how they surprisingly performed miracles, healed people, preached, and spoke in tongues. Things that they had not been able to do in such measure prior to the Holy Spirit's coming and outside of their relationship with Jesus Christ.

"But you shall receive power when the Holy Spirit has come upon you; and you shall be witnesses to Me in Jerusalem, and in all Judea and Samaria, and to the end of the earth" (Acts 1:8). The power (δύναμιν) they were to receive is the very same power that Jesus had when He walked this earth. Besides, when the Holy Spirit came, He didn't leave any gifts behind in heaven. All authority (ἐξουσία) and all power was given to Jesus and then passed on to His Church (Matthew 28:18).

With the precious gift of the Holy Spirit came resurrection power, and with His spiritual gifts came a supernatural empowerment for all believers to continue the ministry of Jesus until He comes. No one should ever underestimate the power and anointing behind the nine Gifts of the Holy Spirit. They were not given because they have no value or have passed their sell-by date! They were given to equip and empower believers to do and act like Jesus. The Body of Christ should truly treasure these gifts. For no one but God Himself would have been able to allocate them fittingly. Romans 12:3-8 and 1 Corinthians chapter 12 make it clear that each Christian is given spiritual gifts according to God's divine choice. We are also told in

1 Corinthians 12:28-31 and in 1 Corinthians 14:12-13 that it is God alone who selects the gifts.

These passages also indicate that not everyone will manifest a particular gift. Paul tells the Corinthian believers that if they are going to desire spiritual gifts, they should strive after the more edifying gifts, such as prophesying (speaking forth the word of God for the edifying of other believers). But the most important thing to grasp is the fact that they are all spiritual gifts. They are all supernatural! Freely given by God, and freely operated by the Holy Spirit ("as He wills"). The human mind cannot comprehend the enormity of what God has given His Church. "Eye has not seen, nor ear heard, nor have entered into the heart of man. The things which God has prepared for those who love Him" (1 Corinthians 2:9).

Because of the Gifts of the Holy Spirit, and the spiritual aids that accompany Him, there is now an out-flowing of God's Spirit from the life of every believer (in different measures and degrees). Someone once said, "The highest capacity of man was the ability to contain God." Is our highest capacity, the ability to contain God? Or, is the highest capacity when God's Spirit flows out from our lives? We are chosen channels through which God can pour out His love (and His power) to the destitute world that surrounds us. In John 7:37-39, Jesus declared, "If anyone thirsts, let him come to Me and drink. He who believes in Me, as the Scripture has said, out of his heart will flow rivers of living water." However, this He spoke concerning the Spirit, whom those believing in Him would receive; for the Holy Spirit was not yet given because Jesus was not yet glorified.

It is very likely that this is what Jesus was directing His disciples toward. It is not just the "indwelling" of the Holy Spirit (inside a believer), as marvellous as that is, but the releasing of the Spirit's power and presence from within.

This is when a torrent of living water begins to flow out of the lives of Christians so that the world around them is affected by what God has done in them. As a result, they are drawn to Christ.

The one principle is subjective. It is the Holy Spirit continually at work within – transforming believers into the very image of Jesus Christ. However, it's always toward the objective when impartation becomes instigation. When Christians become instruments through which God can touch a lost and dying world. In his letter to the Corinthians, chapters 12 through 14, Paul is describing some of the ways by which the Spirit of God is manifested in the Church and revealed through the lives of its members. First of all, in the early part of chapter 12, he gives a listing of the nine various operations, which he declares the Holy Spirit divides to each man severally as He wills. Not all members of the Body of Christ possess all of these manifestations. As he closes out the twelfth chapter, Paul asks these rhetorical questions: Are all apostles? Are all prophets? Are all teachers? Are all workers of miracles? Have all the gifts of healing? do all speak with tongues? Do all interpret? (1 Corinthians 12:29-30). The answer is clearly, "no." The Holy Spirit divides to each man severally as He wills. When put together correctly, we visibly see the whole Body of Christ functioning as God would have the body to function – "as one."

It is this functionality, when every member of the Body of Christ is being well-matched to serve a divine purpose, which causes the Church to grow into the glorious Bride that Jesus is coming back for (Ephesians 5:27). A spiritual bride for a spiritual groom!

2

Concerning the Spiritual

"Without some knowledge of Greek, you cannot understand the critical commentaries on the Scriptures, and a commentary that is not critical is of doubtful value."

George Ricker Berry
(Author of the Interlinear Greek to English New Testament)

The Greek language is accurate and very descriptive; it has the unique ability to express thoughts, ideas and concepts precisely and concisely. We are probably all familiar with the saying "the Greeks have a word for it!" In the context of New Testament scripture, I believe this to be true. It would be unwise and ill-advised to assume that any Greek word can be translated (throughout the Bible) using the same English word. Take, for instance, the word "master." This word "master" is used in the Authorised Version to translate *six* different Greek words, all bearing different shades of connotation. The word "judgment" stands for *eight* different Greek words in the original; and so of many others. Consequently, any English translation will only be able to provide a *word* that is the nearest *'literal'* equivalent and can often be misleading in its spiritual application.

The Apostle Paul wrote much of the New Testament, and his depth of thinking and depth of feeling is expressed so beautifully in the original text. His mastery of the Greek language literally parts the clouds and allows the brilliance of our Lord Jesus Christ to shine through in almost every verse. Many times the intensity of Paul's devotion to Christ Jesus, and the sheer force of his commitment, has challenged me to seek more insight and dig deeper. He is truly inspirational and a founder of Christianity.

I have also been astounded by Paul's precise use of words, often borrowed from the secular arena and on occasion only used once in order to make a specific point. I am convinced that this kind of supreme brilliance could only originate in God the Father and that the Holy Spirit Himself must have imparted it to Paul. Likewise, I pray:

> The God of our Lord Jesus Christ, the Father of glory, may give to you the spirit of wisdom and revelation in the knowledge of Him, that the eyes of your understanding being enlightened; that you may know what is the hope of His calling, what are the riches of the glory of His inheritance in the saints, and what is the exceeding greatness of His power toward us who believe, according to the working of His mighty power which He worked in Christ when He raised Him from the dead and seated Him at His right hand in the heavenly places, far above all principality and power and might and dominion, and every name that is named, not only in this age but also in that which is to come. (Ephesians 1:17-21).

Concerning the spiritual (1 Corinthians 12:1), and the **Gifts of the Holy Spirit** (1 Corinthians 12:8-10), I would like to point out from the outset that it doesn't say "gifts of the Church", it says Gifts of the Holy Spirit. There's a big difference. Most people think they are *gifts* of the Church, and that any church can do with them as it pleases but not so! The Church is the recipient - not the benefactor and the *gifts* are implemented "as He wills."

Before Jesus went to the cross, and ascended to the right hand of God, He actually spoke about the Holy Spirit. In fact, He boldly declared, *"Most assuredly, I say to you, he who believes in Me, the **works** that I do he will do also; and **greater works** than these he will do, because I go to My Father"* (John 14:12). Jesus was preparing the Church for the Holy Spirit's coming. On His arrival, on the day of Pentecost, the power of God (in the Person of the Holy Spirit) came to equip the Church to do the very things that Jesus had done.

Again, in John 14:25-26, Jesus openly declares, *"These things I have spoken to you while being present with you. But the **Helper** (παράκλητος), the Holy Spirit, whom the Father will send in My name, He will teach you all things, and bring to your remembrance all things that I said to you."* In John 16:7, the Lord states, *"It is profitable for you that I go away; for if I do not go away, the **Comforter** (παράκλητος) will not come to you; but if I go I will send Him to you."* Further, in John 16:13-15, we are told,

> However, when He, **the Spirit of truth**, has come, He will guide you into all truth; for He will not speak on His own authority, but whatever He hears He will speak; and He will tell you things to come. He will glorify Me, for He will take of what is Mine and declare it to you. All things that the Father has are Mine. Therefore, I said that He will take of Mine and declare it to you.

From the outset, Jesus intended to go and send us the Holy Spirit. God's Spirit is not a puff of smoke or some sort of mystical figure, He is a real person. The Greek word there παράκλμτος (another Helper), is someone who draws along-side and basically does exactly what Jesus would do if he was present. The Holy Spirit is the third Person in the Godhead – He is the only Person who can represent Jesus in the most perfect and complete way here on earth.

Furthermore, He was sent with a distinct purpose, and that is, to teach believers and guide them into **all truth**. The Bible also says that He will bring glory to Jesus! What we need to understand concerning the Holy Spirit and His gifts, when they are operating in the church, is that they are meant to bring glory to Jesus. The *gifts* should never bring glory to man, or draw attention to man. Anyone who desires to operate in the Gifts of the Holy Spirit must be totally focused on

Jesus getting all the glory. A Christian should be doing everything he/she can to glorify Jesus. Only then is the Holy Spirit obliged to use them. Why? Because His singular directive is "to bring glory to Jesus."

In 1 Corinthians 14:12, it tells us to be zealous for spiritual gifts. *"Even so you, since you are zealous of spiritual gifts, seek that you may excel to the edifying of the church."* This is probably where 90% of the Body of Christ will get disqualified. The Holy Spirit is constantly seeking passionate, enthusiastic, ambitious people through which He can manifest His *spiritual gifts.* What's more, if a believer wants to outshine others in the process of building up the church, he/she needs to be zealous - have the energy and the desire. Imagine being able to do what Jesus would do if He was present! Well, this is possible with the help and guidance of God's Spirit. He is a wonderful instructor.

When re-examining the **Gifts of the Holy Spirit**, having taught on the subject many times in the past, I felt compelled to go back to the original Greek text. What the Holy Spirit revealed to me was truly astounding! It was so encouraging that I wanted to capture it in 'book form' for people to read, study and enjoy at their leisure.

1 Corinthians 12

The first thing that stands out, when examining this passage of scripture in the original Greek is the emphasis on the Holy Spirit rather than His gifts. What's also openly communicated is the prerequisite to submit to God's Spirit before any of His gifts can be manifest. I noticed that the word "in" is strategically placed to suggest *"in submission to,"* or *"under the influence of."* For example, in verse 8, it says, *"For to one truly indeed, in the Spirit, is given a word of wisdom; to another, a word of knowledge, according to the same Spirit."* Implying, *"For to one truly indeed, in submission to the Spirit, is given a word of wisdom; to another, a word of knowledge, according to the same Spirit."* Another way of rightfully discerning this spiritual principle is by accepting that *submission and obedience* are part of the same process.

Throughout the Bible, *submission* and *obedience* can be found working together. When Jesus told His disciples not to depart from Jerusalem but wait for the promise of the Father (Acts 1:4), they **obeyed** His command and waited in the Upper Room for the coming of the Spirit. It was out of that obedience that they were then *filled* with the Holy Spirit (Acts 2:4). Obedience led to surrender which, in turn, caused God's **power** to be released. Therefore, the Gifts of the Holy Spirit only manifest when the vessel God intends to use is in total submission – under the complete influence of the Spirit of God.

Concerning 1 Corinthians 12, here is what I discovered - through my personal understanding of the original Greek...

1.   Περὶ δὲ τῶν πνευματικῶν, ἀδελφοί, οὐ θέλω ὑμᾶς ἀγνοεῖν.

"Furthermore, concerning the spiritual, brothers, I do not want you to be ignorant."

There is no mention of "gifts" as most translations suggest. It simply refers to "the spiritual." Due to the fact that the church in Corinth needed instruction concerning what was (or was not) spiritual, the apostle Paul decided to start this passage with a warning, "Concerning the spiritual, I don't want you to be ill-informed." All the verses following this statement are written to inform the Corinthians as to what is truly spiritual.

2.   Οἴδατε ὅτι ὅτε ἔθνη ἦτε πρὸς τὰ εἴδωλα τὰ ἄθωνα ὡς ἂν ἤγεσθε ἀπαγόμενοι.

"You know that when you were pagans, even as (anyhow) you were led away to mute idols, (always) being led astray."

The Corinthians are reminded of their pagan past, to let them know how easy it was for them to be led astray by false spirituality. A warning concerning their predisposition to be influenced by idolatry. What is in fact without life or power.

3.   διὸ γνωρίζω ὑμῖν ὅτι οὐδεὶς ἐν Πνεύματι Θεοῦ λαλῶν λέγει ᾿Ανάθεμα ᾿Ιησοῦς, καὶ οὐδεὶς δύναται εἰπεῖν, Κύριος᾿Ιησοῦς, εἰ μὴ ἐν πνεύματι ἁγίῳ.

"Therefore, I make known to you that no one, speaking in the Spirit of God, says accursed is Jesus; and no one is able to say, Jesus is Lord, if not in the Holy Spirit."

Here, Paul confirms a fundamental truth. That no one speaking in submission to the Spirit can blaspheme against Jesus, and no one is able to confess Jesus is Lord, except under the influence of the Holy Spirit. The Holy Spirit will always motivate and inspire believers to exalt Jesus and place Him above all else! *For He alone is worthy to receive honour, and glory and power, for ever and ever* (Revelation 5:13).

4.   Διαιρέσεις δὲ χαρισμάτων εἰσίν, τὸ δὲ αὐτὸ πνεῦμα·

"Besides, there are varieties of gifts, but the same Spirit;"

The Holy Spirit's ministry is very diverse, and so too are His gifts. The Spirit's gifts have the unique quality of being always fresh. And there is an absence of uniformity. Why? Because He may manifest the same gift, but it will never be at the same time, in the same manner, within the same means. All the spiritual gifts mentioned are entirely diverse in operation and manifestation. However, they are all controlled and released by the same Spirit.

5.   καὶ διαιρέσεις διακονιῶν εἰσι, καὶ ὁ αὐτὸς κύριος·

"And there are varieties of services, but the same Lord;"

This verse is probably referring to the distribution of ministry gifts (administrations) as mentioned in Romans 12:4-8:

For as we have many members in one body, but all the members do not have the same function, so we, being many, are one body in Christ, and individually members of one another. Having then gifts differing according to the grace that is given to us, let us use them: if prophecy, let us prophesy in proportion to our faith; or ministry, let us use it in our ministering; he who teaches, in teaching; he who exhorts, in exhortation; he who gives, with liberality; he who leads, with diligence; he who shows mercy, with cheerfulness.

6.   καὶ διαιρέσεις ἐνερλημάτων εἰσίν, ὁ δὲ αὐτὸς Θεός, ὁ ἐνεργῶν τὰ πάντα ἐν πᾶσιν.

"And there are varieties of workings, but the same God is working all things (always) in everyone."

There are diversities of operations but the same God. In these three verses, we can clearly see the doctrine of the Holy Trinity. The gifts are attributed to the Spirit (verse 4); administrations to the Lord Jesus (verse 5); and operations to God the Father (verse 6). There are different operations in the mind of God and different powers distributed to man. Additionally, there are different methods in building up the church but the same Father! They should not therefore, be undervalued; nor should anyone be unduly elated or pride himself on what has been conferred by God alone. All these operations should always be traced back to Him.

7.   ἑκάστῳ δὲ δίδοται ἡ φανέρωσις τοῦ πνεύματος πρὸς τὸ συμφέρον.

"What's more, to each is given the manifestation of the Spirit for the common profiting."

What Paul means here is this: Whatever gifts God has bestowed, or in whatever manner the Holy Spirit may choose to manifest Himself, it is all for the common benefit of the Church. God has given no gift to any man for his exclusive use or for his own private improvement. He has been given it for the **common good** and benefit of others. Therefore, all Christians should employ their time, gifts and talents for the common welfare of others and for the advancement of the kingdom of God here on earth.

8.   ᾧ μὲν γὰρ διὰ τοῦ πνεύματος δίδοται λόγος σοφίας, ἄλλῳ δὲ λόγος γνώσεως κατὰ τὸ αὐτὸ πνεῦμα,

"For to one truly indeed, in the Spirit, is given a word of wisdom; to another, a word of knowledge, according to the same Spirit;"

Here, the apostle Paul starts listing the nine Gifts of the Holy Spirit, and notice how he begins with the statement, "for to one truly indeed." Emphasising how individually valuable each gift is. The gifts respectively have two main characteristics (1) they are under the influence of God's Spirit, and (2) they are bestowed exclusive by God's Spirit.

9. ἑτέρῳ πίστις ἐν τῷ αὐτῷ πνεύματι, ἄλλῳ δὲ χαρίσματα ἰαμάτων ἐν τῷ ἑνὶ πνεύματι,

"And to a different one, faith, by the same Spirit; but to another gifts of healings, in the same Spirit;"

Again, this verse is highlighting the uniqueness of the gifts and the exclusivity given to the Holy Spirit. The Greek word ἄλλῳ (translated "another") is literally 'a distinct and unique other'.

10. ἄλλῳ δὲ ἐνεργήματα δυνάμεων, ἄλλῳ [δὲ] προφητεία, ἄλλῳ [δὲ] διακρίσεις πνευμάτων, ἑτέρῳ γένη γλωσσῶν, ἄλλῳ δὲ ἑρμηνεία γλωσσῶν·

"Moreover to another, working of miracles; again, to another prophecy; to another, discerning of spirits; and to a different one, various kinds of tongues; likewise to another, interpretation of tongues."

Here we find ἄλλῳ ('another') repeated four times. Dividing each of the gifts mentioned by their divine distinctiveness.

11. πάντα δὲ ταῦτα ἐνεργεῖ τὸ ἓν καὶ τὸ αὐτὸ πνεῦμα, διαιροῦν ἰδίᾳ ἑκάστῳ καθὼς βούλεται.

"But all these things (always) works the one and the self-same Spirit, apportioning personally to each as He wills."

Again, in contrast to the great varieties of gifts, the **common** source of them all is emphatically repeated. There are three reassuring facts mentioned here: (1) The Holy Spirit is always at work, producing and manifesting the right gift; (2) in doing so, He assigns and divides the gifts personally – 'one on one'; (3) and the manifestation of each gift is distributed as He sees fit.

12. Καθάπερ γὰρ τὸ σῶμα ἕν ἐστιν καὶ μέλη πολλὰ ἔχει, πάντα δὲ τὰ μέλη τοῦ σώματος πολλὰ ὄντα ἕν ἐστιν σῶμα, οὕτως καὶ ὁ Χριστός·

"For even as the body is one and has many members, but all the members of that body being many, are one body, so also is Christ."

Matthew Henry's Concise Commentary undoubtedly provides the best explanation of these next two verses. "Christ and His church form one body, as Head and members. Christians become members of this body by baptism. The outward rite is of Divine institution; it is a sign of the new birth, and is called therefore the washing of regeneration, Titus 3:5. But it is by the Spirit, only by the renewing of the Holy Ghost, that we are made members of Christ's body. And by communion with Christ at the Lord's supper, we are strengthened, not by drinking the wine, but by drinking into one Spirit. Each member has its form, place, and use. The lowliest makes a part of the body. There must be a distinction of members in the body.

So Christ's members have different powers and different places. We should do the duties of our own place in the church, and not murmur, or quarrel with others. All the members of the body are useful and necessary to each other. Nor is there a member of the body of Christ, who may and ought not to be useful to fellow-members. As in the natural body of man, the members should be closely united by the strongest bonds of love; the good of the whole should be the object of all. All Christians are dependent one upon another; each is to expect and receive help from the rest. Let us then have more of the spirit of union in our religion".

13. καὶ γὰρ ἐν ἑνὶ πνεύματι ἡμεῖς πάντες εἰς ἓν σῶμα ἐβαπτίσθημεν, εἴτε Ἰουδαῖοι εἴτε Ἕλληνες, εἴτε δοῦλοι εἴτε ἐλεύθεροι, καὶ πάντες ἓν πνεῦμα ἐποτίσθημεν.

"Also indeed, in one Spirit, we were all baptised into one body, whether Jews or Greeks, whether slaves or free, and all one Spirit we were made to drink."

Further to what has been so meaningfully written in Matthew Henry's commentary above, we must acknowledge the absolute necessity for **unity** - "in one Spirit." No matter what nation you represent, what language you speak, or what position you hold in life, you must realise that we were all created to partake of the **same Spirit**. The Spirit of 'ἑνότης' - oneness!

Now that I have explained these 13 verses, from the original Greek text of 1 Corinthians 12, let us examine the nine Gifts of the Holy Spirit in depth...

3

The Word of Wisdom

ᾧ μὲν γὰρ διὰ τοῦ πνεύματος δίδοται λόγος σοφίας

"For to one truly indeed, in the Spirit, is given
a Word of Wisdom"

When studying the Gifts of the Holy Spirit, it is important to note that they appear in a deliberate and specific order. Many scholars divide them up into three groups of three. That is, gifts that "reveal" something (*the revelation gifts*), gifts that "do" something (*the power gifts*), and gifts the "say" something (*the vocal gifts*). However, I do not agree with this approach because it implies that the Holy Spirit couldn't divide His nine gifts up into groups Himself, or that maybe the apostle Paul was in error when documenting these *spiritual gifts*.

The fact is, if God wanted to have us study them in a different order, He would have listed them accordingly. The nine Gifts of the Holy Spirit, as detailed in 1 Corinthians 12, **do** appear in the right order and in the correct verses. We will be able to see why as we dig deeper. So let us start with the first gift mentioned...

The **Word of Wisdom** is probably the most essential gift but not the most important. That is why it is mentioned first. The most important (or greatest) gift is the one that is necessary at that exact time, in that specific location, for that particular person.

The Word of Wisdom is however essential if any of the other eight gifts are to be applied or performed correctly. Remember, these are *supernatural gifts* that the Holy Spirit is manifesting through human vessels. Therefore, we need **wisdom** to know 'what', 'when' and 'how' to collaborate with the Spirit of God so that the Church may be edified (built up). There are an infinite number of possibilities where you will need God's wisdom to navigate safely though the issues confronting you. Again, since human intelligence is so limited in its ability to apply real wisdom to solve life's challenges, we all need the *wisdom of God* flowing through our lives like a river. There is no better way to handle and overcome adversity.

So, what exactly is the Gift of the Word of Wisdom? It is *'the application of all knowledge received direct from the Holy Spirit'*. This is not natural knowledge because it does not come through the five senses – it comes direct from God. Such **wisdom** is simply a human vessel applying knowledge *'with God's skill and ability'*. It is crucial for believers to seek the Word of Wisdom and pray to receive it continually. If you sincerely desire this *gift*, you should ask God to saturate your life with it. A Word of Wisdom can illuminate your understanding at any time. That way you will know how to cope with, and handle, the more complex and unforeseen problems you may encounter.

In 1 Corinthians 12:8, "word" in Word of Wisdom is translated from the Greek word 'logos' (λόγος from λέγω - *"I say"*) meaning *'the spoken word; the word spoken, not written'*.

The word 'λόγος' (logos) is to speak in such a way as to *build up*, *bless* and cause others to *prosper*. That's what the Gifts of the Spirit are all about. They are not meant to pull down people, or be used in a way that criticises individuals, or condemns a body of believers. Therefore, whatever is spoken (or declared) under the influence of God's Spirit will build up and edify the listener – and nothing else!

The word "wisdom" comes from the Greek word 'σοφία' (sofia) and it means:

- *cleverness, skill; a right application of knowledge; the ability, or result of an ability, to think and act utilizing knowledge, common sense, understanding, and insight;*

- *supreme intelligence such as belongs to God, broad and full of intelligence (used of the knowledge of very diverse matter), the varied knowledge of things human and divine, acquired by acuteness and experience, the act of interpreting dreams and always giving sound advice, skill in the management of human affairs, skill and discretion in imparting Christian truth, the knowledge and practice of the requisites for godly and upright living.*

The well-known commentator, William Barclay, has this to say on the **Word of Wisdom**: "Clement of Alexandria defined 'σοφία' as *'the knowledge of things human and divine and of their causes.'* Aristotle described it as *'striving after the best ends and using the best means.'* This is the highest kind of wisdom; and it comes not so much from thought as *from communion with God. It is the wisdom which knows God."*

Spiritual wisdom ('σοφία'), is also defined as the power to confirm and to commend the truth with wise and intelligent reasoning (once it has been intuitively grasped). So, 'σοφία' is available for the Church to receive a clear-sighted instruction which can act for the best interests of all - in any given situation. It is a wisdom that will intuitively recognize and grasp the truth. It's a wisdom that makes the truth intelligible to the thinking mind and persuasively commends it to others.

However, there are two words that appear in the New Testament and are translated 'wisdom'. The first, 'σοφία', which we have just examined. But there is another, 'φρόνησις' (phronesis). 'Σοφία' implies *'a God given special insight into the true nature and state of things or situations'*. Whereas, 'phronesis' is *'the practical and sensible use of such insight (the right use of the mind)'*.

'Phronesis' is literally an understanding that leads to right action. It is used in Luke 1:17,

> He will be a man with the spirit and power of Elijah. He will prepare the people for the coming of the Lord. He will turn the hearts of the fathers to their children, and He will cause those who are rebellious to accept the wisdom of the godly.

The word 'φρόνησις' is concerned with how to act in particular situations. One can learn the principles of action but applying them in the real world, in situations one could not have foreseen, requires a certain kind of wisdom. Quite simply, 'σοφία' has spiritual qualities, but 'φρόνησις' is purely practical. Therefore, I firmly believe that God's wisdom (or the God kind of wisdom) must incorporate both 'σοφία' and 'φρόνησις'. In other words, God's **wisdom**; (a) *gives us* **spiritual** *insight into the true nature and state of things,* and (b) *it causes us to apply a sensible and reasonable approach to the* **practical** *use of such insight.*

Notice something? If we were only blessed with spiritual insight and had no practical ability to apply it in our lives, it would be of no value to us - or to anybody else! Possessing the "mind of Christ" may have many spiritual attributes, but it should also have practical and sensible applications. Colossians 4:5 tells us to *"walk in wisdom toward those who are on the outside"* (the unbelievers). This cannot be a purely spiritual experience, for we know that the lost are unable to comprehend the things of the Spirit, for they are not spiritually minded.

What's quite obvious is this... Though the word 'sophia' is used in relation to the Gifts of the Holy Spirit, the manifestation and application of the *gifts* will include 'phronesis'. Why? Because there is always a practical application with any *gift* (as listed in 1 Corinthians 12). The Church has need of both types of **wisdom**. (1) A type of wisdom that pertains to spiritual matters, and (2) a type of wisdom that relates to practical things. Resulting in an **ability** to discern how (or why) to act properly, and encourage others to do the same. Thus, producing excellence of character and spiritual maturity.

The gift of the Word of Wisdom enables a believer to express the Holy Spirit's revelation, knowledge or answers to either an individual or to a group of people, in a way that surpasses any previous "human ability". It is the supernatural impartation of facts, and it is not "natural." This gift involves having a sense of **divine direction**, being led by the Holy Spirit to act appropriately in a given set of circumstances. It carries the hallmark of the Wisdom of God. It carries His very DNA! And God's wisdom beats all the other kinds of wisdom known to man. It rules supreme!

The Characteristics of Wisdom from God

Remember, we are incapable of applying God's wisdom except through His divine nature. That is why we must always be able to recognise the Wisdom of God. For, whatever is said through the manifestation of the Gift of the Word of Wisdom will fully comply to the characteristics of *divine wisdom.*

James, the brother of Jesus, identifies all the characteristics of divine wisdom. In James 3:17 he says: *"But the wisdom that is from above is first pure, then peaceable, gentle, willing to reason, full of mercy and good fruits, without partiality and without hypocrisy."* We can learn much about the characteristics of **wisdom** from this verse of scripture:

1. Wisdom is *"From Above."* Therefore, it is not already in the earth. Wisdom is something over which we have no control. Wisdom is a gift given as God sees fit but just because it is a gift, does not mean we shouldn't seek after it or desire it.

2. Wisdom is *"Pure."* It is holy and it is pure! The Greek for "pure" used here is 'ἁγνός' meaning 'innocent, modest and perfect'.

3. Wisdom is "Peaceable." The Greek is 'εἰρηνικός', meaning 'peaceable, agreeable and tranquil'. It also implies, 'loving peace, bringing peace with it, and being peaceful'. The wisdom of God, therefore, does not bring fear, or worry or unnecessary concern.

4. Wisdom is *"Gentle."* It is meek, modest, kind, and is not self-attention grabbing. The Greek word 'ἐπιεικής' means *'mild, gentle, in moderation, patient, suitable, equitable, and fair'.*

5. Wisdom is *"Willing to Reason."* It's not stubborn, or obstinate but yielding to others, easily compatible and approachable (all from the Greek word 'εὐπειθής'). It also infers, *'open to reason, and a yielding disposition in all indifferent things.*

6. Wisdom is *"Full of Mercy."* It's ready to pass by an offence and grant forgiveness to those who transgress - performing every possible act of kindness and practical help. The Greek word 'ἔλεος' literally means *'kindness or good will towards the miserable and afflicted'* (joined with a desire to help).

7. Wisdom is *"Full of Good Fruits."* Good fruits, 'καρπός' also means good deeds - the fruits of righteousness (Philippians 1:11), including those listed in Galatians 5:22-23, *"The fruit of the Spirit is: love, joy, peace, long-suffering, kindness, goodness, faith, meekness, self-control; against such things there is no law."*

8. Wisdom is *"Impartial"* - without partiality and being of no respect to persons. The Greek word 'ἀδιάκριτος' also means 'without dubiousness, ambiguity or uncertainty'. It is clear that God's wisdom does not pander to the man, or a person's celebrity status, or financial means.

9. Wisdom is *"Without Hypocrisy"* and sincere. The Greek word 'ἀνυπόκριτος' (used here) means *'genuine, open, undisguised, unaffected'.* Simply, *'not putting on an act, with respect to God or man'.*

Therefore, whenever the Holy Spirit demonstrates His gifts, the **divine character** will express itself (through the operation of that specific gift). However, if we are not acquainted with the features and characteristics of the divine nature we won't be able to correctly discern the Spirit, and consequently, this may hinder us from becoming vessels for God's glory. Every spiritual gift "in action" will always bring glory to God.

To assist us in sharing the other Gifts of the Spirit correctly and in edifying the Church, the **Word of Wisdom** is indispensable in our daily lives. For instance, it's one thing to receive a *word of prophecy, knowledge, faith, healing,* etc., yet it is completely different to delivering that gift in such a way as to allow it to have its fullest impact – uncontaminated by human opinion. Many believers do in fact receive spiritual information, as with the Gifts of the Holy Spirit, but they do not always know how to convey them. If we do not minister in the Wisdom of God, we will make mistakes. We may even breed contempt and bring dishonour to the *gifts,* which is what was happening in the church in Corinth. Insensitivity to the person or people we are conveying the information to, can be a serious problem. The *spiritual gift* may be correct, but the manner of dispensing it may be incorrect. The Word of Wisdom will always ensure that the *gift* is delivered flawlessly - *"the right application of knowledge."*

In Jesus' account of the "Wise and Foolish Builders," both men had built their houses - one on a rock, the other on the sand – but only the wise man rightly applied the words of Jesus. The foolish man heard exactly the same words, from the mouth of the same Jesus, but did not apply them correctly. And as a result, he came to ruin (Matthew 7:24-27; Luke 6:46-49). The Word of Wisdom comes directly from the mouth of Jesus (via the Holy Spirit), so let's make sure we are listening and acting accordingly!

Some Examples of the Word of Wisdom

In 1 Kings 3:16–28 we find an account of King Solomon hearing a case involving two prostitutes. The two women had both recently given birth to sons, and they lived together in the same home. During the night, one of the infants was smothered and died.

The woman whose son had died switched her dead baby with the baby of the other woman as she slept. The other woman, seeking justice, took the matter before the king. She stated her case:

We were alone; there was no one in the house but the two of us. During the night this woman's son died because she lay on him. So she got up in the middle of the night and took my son from my side while I your servant was asleep. She put him by her breast and put her dead son by my breast. The next morning, I got up to nurse my son—and he was dead! But when I looked at him closely in the morning light, I saw that it wasn't the son I had borne. (verses 18–21).

Solomon could not tell from their words which woman was telling the truth. Instead, he issued a shocking command: *"Bring me a sword... Cut the living child in two and give half to one and half to the other"* (1 Kings 3:24–25). After he said this, the woman whose son was still alive said, *"Please, my lord, give her the living baby! Don't kill him!"* However, the other woman, whose son had died, answered, *"Neither I nor you shall have him. Cut him in two!"* (verse 26). Based on their responses, Solomon knew the identity of the true mother: *"Give the living baby to the first woman. Do not kill him; she is his mother"* (verse 27).

The chapter's final verse documents the effect that Solomon's unorthodox methods had on the kingdom: *"When all Israel heard the verdict the king had given, they held the king in awe, because they saw that he had **wisdom from God** to administer justice"* (1 Kings 3:28). Solomon's wisdom had been given by God when Solomon requested it (verse 5). The account of Solomon's handling of the case of the two prostitutes showed that he had indeed been granted Wisdom from God.

Another example is found in Acts 16. As Paul's missions team was going to the place of prayer, probably to give further teaching to these new believers, a slave girl with a spirit of divination met them. The Greek word makes clear that this was a girl, not a grown woman. There were more than sixty million slaves in the Roman Empire - men, women, and children who were denied all their civil rights. This slave-girl's masters were getting rich, at her expense, through her fortune-telling.

Now, this girl has what Luke calls a "spirit of divination." The literal Greek reads, *"she had a spirit of a python,"* which is the same term used for a 'python snake'. And this referred to the legendary snake in Greek mythology that guarded the Delphic Oracle in Central Greece. Apollo supposedly killed this snake, and the snake's spirit then resided in the priestess. So a "python spirit" characterises a spirit that enables someone to predict the future. Such people generally spoke with their mouths closed, uttering words completely out of their control, and therefore, they became known as *"ventriloquists."*

The girl mentioned was just one of the thousands of priestesses from the ancient city of Delphi who were called "pythons" because they were connected to Apollo. She was seen as having contact with the gods and also as being able to foresee the future. It seems that the slave-girl could actually see into the future, and that is why her owners earned so much money from her. But the power really came from satan - by an evil spirit that controlled her speech. Acts 16 says the girl was possessed by a demon:

> This girl followed Paul and us, and cried out, saying, *"These men are the servants of the Most High God, who proclaim to us the way of salvation."* And this she did for many days.
>
> But Paul, greatly annoyed, turned and said to the spirit, *"I command you in the name of Jesus Christ to come out of her."* And he came out that very hour.* (Acts 16:17-18)

The python demon (pneuma pythona) within the slave-girl knew of Paul and announced through her "who he was and what he was doing." Paul's response was the same as the response Jesus had to a demon-possessed man in the synagogue at Capernaum. This man had said to the Lord, *"I know who you are, the Holy One of God..."* As with Jesus, the apostle Paul did not want this kind of message coming from a demon-possessed person in case the people would think that his own proclamation of the Gospel was in some way associated with satan.

"Paul was greatly annoyed..." The word in Greek is not really "annoyed," for that makes it sound as if he were merely irritated by this woman who kept following him around. The word means, he

was *"deeply troubled."* So, Paul turned around and said to the spirit (not to the girl), *"I command you in the name of Jesus Christ to come out of her!"* The results are immediate. *"And it came out at that very moment."* The python demon obeyed the words of Paul! Here Luke is demonstrating Paul's authority over the *fallen spirit* world. What we see here are servants of the Most High God defeating a python spirit - revealing that Jesus was more powerful than Apollo.

Nonetheless, timing was everything! Why did Paul choose that exact moment to deal with the evil spirit? The girl had been following him *"for many days."* Yes, he may have been deeply troubled, but that was probably true from the start. Paul chose that moment because he was **influenced** by the Holy Spirit. The gift of the Word of Wisdom was in operation.

Notice, Paul did not rush in straightaway and deliver the girl. He waited "many days" before confronting it. That was wisdom! However, this illustration does not mean that a similar case would necessarily be handled in the same way. We may need to act today, or tomorrow, next week, next month, or even next year. Wisdom always gets the timing right!

In Acts 5:1-11, Peter used the Word of Wisdom to make sure that both Ananias and Sapphira exposed their own evil doings and so suffered the consequences of their own actions. He did not accuse Sapphira on the confession of her husband alone, but wisely heard from her as well. Then Peter said to her,

> How is it that you have agreed together to test the Spirit of the Lord? Look, the feet of those who have buried your husband are at the door, and they will carry you out." Then immediately she fell down at his feet and breathed her last. And the young men came in and found her dead, and carrying her out, buried her by her husband. So great fear came upon all the church and upon all who heard these things. (verse 9 to 11).

Peter had knowledge of their deceitful dealings but chose to expose them separately.

We should never underestimate the **power** of wisdom. There was a time, when knowledge was power. Knowledge was power back then because so few had it and because so little was known by anyone. Knowledge was power because it was hard to find, hard to access, and hard to understand. However, "in Christ" none of that is true. It has been nullified! *"For God has chosen the foolish things of the world to put to shame the wise"* (1 Corinthians 1:27). *"But of Him you are in Christ Jesus, who became for us wisdom from God"* (verse 30). Yet, it doesn't stop there, "Christ the power of God and the wisdom of God" (verse 24).

*Note, I will provide personal testimonies concerning this gift with examples of the other gifts in operation.

4

The Word of Knowledge

ἄλλῳ δὲ λόγος γνώσεως κατὰ τὸ αὐτὸ πνεῦμα,

"...to another, a word of knowledge, according to the same Spirit;"

Colossians 2:3 says, *"In Christ are hidden all treasures of wisdom and knowledge."* The gift of the Word of Wisdom and the gift of the Word of Knowledge often work together in harmony. The reason being that the Word of Knowledge, when delivered by the Holy Spirit, needs to be correctly applied. For that to happen, the Word of Wisdom must also be active and fully operational. Hence, it is necessary for the Word of Wisdom to work in conjunction with the Word of Knowledge.

There are many different and varied descriptions of the Word of Knowledge. Here are some of them:

- *"It is, the Holy Spirit transmitting His specific information to you on something that you would have no ability or means to be able to know about with your limited levels of knowledge."*

- *"It is, receiving special information directly from God the Father concerning any given situation."*

- *"It is, a knowledge of things that you would not know through a natural attainment or study."*

- *"It is, something that couldn't possibly be known without the Holy Spirit's prompting."*

- *"It is, the supernatural revelation by the Holy Spirit of certain facts in the mind of God."*

- *"It is, the ability to know facts about circumstances or people that could not have been known by natural means."*

- *"It is, a gift that allows you to see a situation as God sees."*

There are numerous examples throughout Scripture where the Word of Knowledge is given by the Holy Spirit - with precise information concerning a specific need or problem. However, I would like to start with an example, through an experience I had, that clearly demonstrates the strong association between the Word of Wisdom and the Word of Knowledge...

I was asked to address a Christian group that met once a week over lunchtime at the IBM Headquarters in South Africa. After I had shared what was on my heart, I looked over and saw a lady standing with a number of people chatting. As I glanced over, I suddenly received comprehensive personal information about this lady (a person I had never met before). It was immediate and very detailed. It was as if God had downloaded, in an instance, what He wanted me to know about this woman. And this was definitely a Word of Knowledge. Nevertheless, I needed to know what to do with the knowledge I had received.

On with my story... What God had shown me was that this lady has been freely sharing her husband with another woman. He would spend the weekdays with his lover and then come home for the weekend. That way it always looked like he was away working. God also showed me that she was only permitting this because she was afraid to lose him and disrupt the family. The Word of Knowledge I received was quite shocking! So I thought to myself, "What must I do with such intimate, and potentially embarrassing, information?" Note, it would have been especially awkward for me if I had got it wrong!

But the Lord is faithful, and He prompted me to go up to her and quietly ask if she would give me a moment of her time. So I asked her if she would step aside from the other people and have a quiet word with me in private. I also told her not to be alarmed as God wanted her to know how much He loved her. Once we were at a safe distance from her friends and colleagues, I looked her in the eye and said, "God has shown me that you are sharing your husband with another woman." I proceeded to give her all the details I had received. As you can imagine, she was shocked! I gently consoled her by reminding her that this was God's way of conveying His love and concern for her.

Then, while we were talking, I received God's remedy for the predicament she was in. God told me to tell her that if she gave her husband an ultimatum, by telling him that she would expose his wicked ways and leave him if necessary, He would heal their marriage. Note, that was a clear demonstration of the Word of Wisdom. Earlier, I had received a Word of Knowledge concerning this lady, intimate details about her marriage, but now I knew what I had to do with that knowledge. And also, the lady knew what she had to do with the "word" I had delivered. Can you see, it's one thing having knowledge, but it's the correct application of the knowledge that brings results.

Fortunately, this story has a happy ending. The lady I had spoken to implemented God's instructions, and He healed the marriage. I didn't receive details of the full outcome until a few months had passed... Initially, the husband tried to resist and emotionally blackmailed his wife. He did everything to make her life so perplexing that she would reconsider and let him carry on with the other woman. Yet, she had supernatural strength and was without fear, therefore, she never compromised. Eventually, God was able to penetrate this man's heart. Subsequently, he repented and apologised to his wife. As it turned out, he was a backslidden believer! After God's intervention, through the Gifts of the Holy Spirit, and some marriage counselling, *this couple fell in love all over again. Most importantly, every member of the family started attending church and are now on fire for God.*

The Gifts of the Holy Spirit may manifest in any situation in your life. This includes; personal, ministry and business affairs. So, as you familiarise yourself with the nine gifts, and the Holy Spirit can trust you with them, they will operate more and more. In my Christian walk and ministry, the spiritual gifts have been effective and totally reliable. We must understand that there are times when only God sees the heart of man, and therefore, we need supernatural intervention.

I was in the music industry for many years. While starting to work full-time for God, I decided to help artists by giving them the benefit of my experience as a record producer and songwriter. I quickly found myself in various roles; as Artist & Repertoire Manager, executive producer and music publisher. In fact, during that time I had a significant amount of "chart" success. One of these Christian artists, whose album I had produced, was signed to my music publishing company. But when the album started to get traction and a song on the album became an international success, something untoward began to brew...

I remember sitting at my desk, going through the mail, when suddenly God dropped something into my spirit. It was as if I was sitting in the bedroom of the leader/songwriter of the group listening to his conversation. I then had spontaneous "knowledge" of what was about to happen, and exactly how I was going to be approached by the leader of that group. Then, as this was going on "in my spirit," the phone rang. It was the leader of the group, wanting to come and see me. So, I told him to come to the office later that day. This would give me enough time to pray about what God wanted me to do with the "knowledge" the Holy Spirit had just imparted to me.

The instruction I received from the Lord was simple, "Give them what they want." After all, the music group was not my source – He was! Consequently, I was fully prepared and totally relaxed with regards the meeting that was set up for later in the day. Hours passed and then the receptionist rang up to say the person I was expecting had arrived. I asked if he could be brought up to my office. When the door opened, I invited him in to take a seat, but he was totally unaware that I already knew why he was there! So, I proceeded to tell him.

This is what I said, "God has already shown me why you wanted to see me and I have all the documents ready." You see, I knew that he was there to ask for his music publishing back so that he may do a deal direct with the major music company that I had introduced him to. At first, he appeared quite startled and baffled. However, what I said next floored him! I said, "You are here to ask for your music publishing back, therefore, I've drawn up an agreement to release you and your copyrights. Once we both sign it, you are free to sign with ---- (the name of the major music company)." I also made it clear that this is what the Lord had instructed me to do, and I was being obedient to His voice. As a result, we will both be blessed!

Again, notice that I was given specific knowledge (a Word of Knowledge) about what was being planned, and then told how to deal with it (a Word of Wisdom). This account can be likened to the story in 2 Kings 6, where Elisha was able to reveal what was going on behind closed doors and secure the victory for the nation of Israel.

...The king of Syria was warring against Samaria and Israel, and the king took counsel with his servants. *"And the man of God sent to the king of Israel, saying, "Beware that you do not pass this place, for the Syrians are coming down there." Then the king of Israel sent someone to the place of which the man of God had told him. Thus, he warned him, and he was watchful there, not just once or twice. Therefore, the heart of the king of Syria was greatly troubled by this thing; and he called his servants and said to them, "Will you not show me which of us is for the king of Israel?" One of his servants said, "None, my lord, O king; but Elisha, the prophet who is in Israel, tells the king of Israel the words that you speak in your bedroom."*

In 2 Kings 5, we also see this gift manifested in the life of Elisha. God would give to Elisha *supernatural knowledge* concerning various things. Remember Naaman, who was a captain of the Syrian army. He had heard that there was a prophet in Israel through whom he could receive a cure of his leprosy. So the king of Syria, who loved this captain very much, sent him with a message to the king of Samaria basically saying, *"Heal my servant, my captain whom I love."* When the king of Samaria got that message he ripped his clothes. He said, *"Look at how this man is trying to antagonise me! I am not God. How can I heal this leper?"* So, Elisha sent a message saying, *"Send him over to me, for that way he will know that there is a prophet of God in Israel."*

So, Naaman came, and Elisha sent his servant out with a message, *"Just go down to the Jordan River and dip in it seven times and you will be cleansed of your leprosy."* This made Naaman very upset. The prophet did not even come out to greet him. He was an important man. Did the prophet not know how important a man he was? And on his way back he was fuming. *"Dip in that muddy Jordan River, are you kidding? We have good, pure, clean rivers up in Damascus. Why should I dip in the Jordan?"* And finally one of Naaman's handmaidens said, *"Well look, what is it going to take? You have come this far, and we are approaching the Jordan River. So it cannot hurt you to give it a try, and who knows, maybe something will happen."* So he was convinced to dip seven times in the Jordan River. And when he came up the seventh time, the leprosy was gone. To his amazement, his skin was normal and he was cured.

Naaman came back to the prophet and sought to reward the prophet of God with great gifts. The prophet said, *"I will not take anything from you"* and just told him to go on his way and rejoice. He made his vow. Naaman said, *"I will serve the God of Israel. He will be the God that I will serve. When I go into the house of Rimmon with my king and I bow my head, I will be bowing my head to the true God. I will fulfil my obligation."* So Naaman made a genuine commitment to God.

Yet you will remember the story... as he was heading back to Syria, Elisha's servant, Gehazi, saw all of the rewards that the prophet had turned down. So, Gehazi decided that he would go and collect these substantial rewards. He went pursuing after Naaman and made up a story. *"After you left a couple of young prophets came along. They needed some help - a little bit of silver and a few changes of clothes,* and so forth." So, Naaman gladly gave it to Gehazi, the servant of Elisha.

We then read in 2 Kings 5:20-27,

> But Gehazi, the servant of Elisha the man of God, said, "Look, my master has spared Naaman this Syrian, while not receiving from his hands what he brought; but as the Lord lives, I will run after him and take something from him." So Gehazi pursued Naaman. When Naaman saw him running after him, he got down from the chariot to meet him, and said, "Is all well?" And he said, "All is well. My master has sent me, saying, 'Indeed, just now two young men of the sons of the prophets have come to me from the mountains of Ephraim. Please give them a talent of silver and two changes of garments.'" So Naaman said, "Please, take two talents." And he urged him, and bound two talents of silver in two bags, with two changes of garments, and handed them to two of his servants; and they carried them on ahead of him. When he came to the citadel, he took them from their hand, and stored them away in the house; then he let the men go, and they departed. Now he went in and stood before his master. Elisha said to him, "Where did you go, Gehazi?" And he said, "Your servant did not go anywhere." Then he said to him, "Did not my heart go with you when the man turned back from his chariot to meet you? Is it time to receive money and to receive clothing, olive groves and vineyards, sheep and oxen, male and female servants? Therefore the leprosy of Naaman shall cling to you and your descendants forever." And he went out from his presence leprous, as white as snow.

Notice, Gehazi did not receive the olive orchards. He did not receive the sheep and the oxen, the vineyards, or the menservants and maidservants. For, this was what he was thinking, "If I just had a couple of talents of silver I could buy me an orchard. I could buy me a vineyard. I could...etc." But the prophet Elisha, having received the Word of knowledge, told him exactly what was going on in his mind - what he was thinking, and what he was planning to do with the money. This is another example of the Word of Knowledge.

We must understand that, the Word of Knowledge is not a *reservoir of knowledge* you can tap into at any time you desire. It is a *divine gift* of God and it often comes at unexpected times. With Elisha this *gift* was demonstrated whenever God wanted to impart "knowledge" of things or "knowledge" of events (*a supernatural knowledge*) to the prophet. However, in 2 Kings 4, when the Shunamite's son had passed out in the field, and he was brought to his mother and died, his mother laid him in the bed and then headed off to confront the prophet of God. She told the servants not to slow down but to get to the prophet as fast as they could. *"Do not slow down! Do not spare for me! Do not worry about me!"*

As the Shunamite woman was approaching the prophet, Elisha looked up and he saw her in the distance, so he sent his servant out to inquire if everything was all right. She said to the servant, "Yes, everything is alright. Get out of the way," and she kept pressing on towards Elisha. So it was, when the man of God saw her afar off, that he said to his servant Gehazi, "Look, the Shunammite woman! Please run now to meet her, and say to her, 'Is it well with you? Is it well with your husband? Is it well with the child?'" And she answered, "It is well." Now when she came to the man of God at the hill, she caught him by the feet, but Gehazi came near to push her away. But the man of God said, "Let her alone; for her soul is in deep distress, and the Lord has hidden it from me, and has not told me" (2 Kings 4:25-27).

Elisha was quite surprised at the fact that there was something desperately wrong and God had not revealed it to him. *"Her spirit is in deep distress, but* **God has not shown me. God has not told me what it was.***"* Therefore, this is not "knowledge" that we tap into at will. It is always "as He chooses" – as He wills!

Observe, it is something that is given to you by God (*a divine revelation or knowledge*). Here, in 2 Kings, Elisha was surprised when the Lord did not show him something. I'm sure most of us are surprised when He does! With Elisha, he was shocked that something was going on and the Lord had not revealed it to him.

In the life of Jesus, we also see this "knowledge" in operation. When Jesus was speaking to the Samaritan woman at the well, He said to her, *"Go, call your husband, and come here."* The woman answered and said, *"I have no husband."* Jesus said to her, *"You have well said, 'I have no husband,' for you have had five husbands, and the one whom you now have is not your husband; in that you spoke truly"* (John 4:16-18). This encounter did not merely transform the woman's life, it got the whole town converted! Think of the ramifications and the possibilities with this gift alone at work. Think of your life if the Holy Spirit Himself were to transmit "divine knowledge" regarding matters that you cannot solve or figure out on your own!

That is why this particular *gift* is so important and so needed in the Church today. Most of us are facing roadblocks or obstacles on regularly in our daily lives. As such, we all need "knowledge" from God flowing through us so we can break through these barriers or obstructions to secure the victory. We also need supernatural "knowledge", if we are to fully accomplish all that the Lord has planned for us – every new assignment He gives us. Wouldn't it be astonishing to see things as God sees them!

The Word of Knowledge is simply the Holy Spirit transmitting specific information to you on something that you would have no ability to know about with your own limited understanding. It is *supernatural* "knowledge" given directly to you by the Holy Spirit and not by your own mind or your own intelligence.

Thinking that you can figure it out on your own is a big mistake, for you only see in part. No one except God sees the complete picture... I was once trying to conclude a large business deal, and it was dragging on and on. The main culprit was a man that we were all constantly struggling with. He was so unpredictable that he repeatedly unnerved the key players and this had a knock-on effect – causing further delays. I had tried all my persuasive skills to get this man to stop being so aggressive and obstreperous but to no avail. He was bent on making all our lives difficult. Then suddenly God imparted "knowledge" about this man that would change everything. God revealed to me that he was a secret alcoholic and that not even his family knew about his addiction.

Armed with this "knowledge", I was able to choose my moment and confront him (in love). Very late one night, I had a call from him and I was sure he had been drinking. Without any thought of the consequences, that is our business relationship and the deal, challenged him. I told him that I knew he was a secret alcoholic and that it was God who had told me. He went really quiet. I then said if God had revealed this to me it was because God wanted to deliver him from his addiction. So, I asked whether he would allow me to pray for him. He said "yes!" After praying for his alcoholism, I immediately asked if we could pray together for his salvation. He agreed, so I led him in a prayer and he surrendered his life to Jesus. Not only did the Word of Knowledge deliver this man from his alcoholism, it blessed his family and his business colleagues also. We concluded our deal and remained friends and Jesus was glorified in everything that had transpired.

It is very important to realise that every *gift* that is activated by the Holy Spirit will bring glory to Jesus. The Word of Knowledge, as with all the Holy Spirit's gifts, are intended to **glorify** Jesus. The Holy Spirit is fully committed to this mission, and He will not release anything unless Jesus Christ is glorified and exalted.

John 16:13-15 confirms this...

> *"However, when He, the Spirit of truth, has come, He will guide you into all truth; for He will not speak on His own authority, but whatever He hears He will speak; and He will tell you things to come. He will glorify Me, for He will take of what is Mine and declare (announce) it to you. All things that the Father has are Mine. Therefore I said that He will take of Mine and declare (announce) it to you."*

What we are told in this passage of scripture is that the Spirit of Truth does not speak on His own authority, and that He will only vocalise what He has already heard. However, the way Jesus is **glorified** is through the process of the Spirit *"taking from what belongs to Jesus and announcing it to us."* Hence, all "knowledge" that is announced by God's Spirit is meant to glorify Jesus Christ. So, whichever gift of the Spirit is imparted through a "word" (the Word of Wisdom or the Word of Knowledge), it is intended to glorify Jesus.

This reminds me of a time when a close friend and colleague of mine had arranged for us to see the leading music distribution company in South Africa. I had just recorded a single with him and we wanted national distribution. We also sought to position ourselves so that the single could enter the charts if possible. I had done some research and discovered that this company was responsible for 60% of sales that qualified a song for chart entry. The reason being, at that time, this company held exclusivity for distribution to all the supermarkets. Anyway, we arrived at the meeting with an unreleased Single in hand and instructions from my colleague to tell the MD of this company about my past successes in the UK (having worked in various capacities with artists such as Cat Stevens and David Bowie; among others).

I remember walking into this man's office, thinking I'm sure he will be impressed with my music industry background. But that was not what God wanted to use, or what God had planned.

Instead of selling the Single, by selling myself, I started to speak prophetically about the company and its future. Before, I could sit down, I looked the head of this major distribution company in the eye and said, "Your company is presently on its knees and we can help you to get up from that place." How presumptuous and rude of me! Yet, because it was God, the man said, "Can I hear the track?" So, we quickly played it, and his response was, "Yes, I would like to run with this." To our amazement, we walked out of the office with a national distribution deal.

But it didn't stop there! God had given me strategy as to how we could get a Christian song into the charts. It was quite simple. I would notify all the churches we were associated with across the country (probably a thousand in total), and ask them to tell their congregations to buy or order our Single, through their local supermarket, during the first week of release. The result was we entered the Top Ten, and therefore, all the radio stations were obliged to play the song and place it on their playlists. Within a few weeks of release we got to number One in the Pop Charts. This opened the door for further releases and even a couple of albums. All of which became Top Ten successes.

Yet, the most important thing for me wasn't chart success. It was God honouring His word to the MD of the distribution company. God said that He would raise the company up from the difficult place it was at, and that's exactly what God did! I found out later, that our success was a turning point in the company's history with regards to music sales. Through a Word of Knowledge (letting me know that the company was in trouble) and a Word of Wisdom (giving us strategy to rescue the company), God was glorified! Christian music (His voice) was able to enter an arena where the majority of contemporary music was being heard. God was able to "speak" to many thousands of unchurched people every day, and the effect was truly astounding!

Our God is never silent. Psalm 50:3 says, *"Our God shall come, and shall **not** keep silent."* Hebrews 1:1-3 declares,

> *"God, who at various times and in various ways spoke in time past to the fathers by the prophets, has in these last days spoken to us by His Son, whom He has appointed heir of all things, through whom also He made the worlds; who being the brightness of His glory and the express image of His person, and **upholding all things by the word of His power."***

If God stopped speaking, all things would fall apart! Why? Because they are being held together by the "word" of His **power**! They are being sustained, preserved, and protected by the "word" of His power! Many times when you hear the voice of God (a "word" concerning your situation,) it serves to protect you from imminent disaster. More importantly, it may even save you from death.

One Sunday, while I was ministering God's word, I glanced over and saw a pregnant woman who had been brought to the service by an Elder in the church. The moment I focused on this young lady, God placed a strong desire in my heart to pray for her baby. This was difficult as I had not finished my message, and I didn't want to alarm the mother of the unborn child. I had no idea why I needed to pray, only that there was an urgency about it. I tried to ignore the inner prompting of the Holy Spirit but I found that I was unable to preach. So, I stepped down from the podium and went across to the young lady – smiling all the way. Under my breath I was speaking to God, saying, "Lord, this is very awkward. What do you want me to say?" Unfortunately I didn't get any further instructions! Therefore, when I was standing in front of the young lady, all I could say was... "Do you mind if I prayed for your baby? Please don't be concerned, all I want to do is speak out a blessing."

Once I started to pray the Holy Spirit began to reveal the reason why I needed to pray and what kind of declaration I needed to make. I then knew, it was a matter of life and death! I kept smiling and asked the mother to put her hand on her tummy. Once she had done this, I placed my hand over her hand and started to pray. For a while I started to pray in the spirit and then spoke out a blessing over both mother and child. I then asked God for His protection over the unborn baby and pleaded the blood of Jesus. Then I declared this scripture, "With long life I will satisfy you" (Psalm 91:16). When I had finished, I looked into the young lady's eyes and expected to see fear and apprehension. Instead, all I could see was a profound peace... "the peace that surpasses all understanding" (Philippians 4:7).

*The service carried on as usual after I had prayed and the young lady left with her friends. A few months later, I heard from the Elder of the church that brought her, what had transpired. The baby was born very prematurely and spent eight weeks in a critical condition. Yet the mother kept reminding herself of what God had declared that Sunday morning. She was able to stand in **faith** for the life of her little girl and see a miracle being fulfilled. The doctors held no hope that the baby would be able to survive, but God's unfailing love was extended to the child even while she was in her mother's womb. Today, I'm sure she has grown into a beautiful young lady.*

Again, the Word of Knowledge, *accompanied* by the Word of Wisdom, was able to accomplish what no doctor was able to. That is, to save the life of an unborn child! Jesus went to the cross that we may live the *'super-abundant life'*. Most of the Gifts of the Holy Spirit are potentially "life-saving." The Bible tells us that *"without knowledge"* we can perish and go into captivity. Many times, only the powerful "knowledge" that comes direct from God can save us or deliver us.

It must be understood that a Word of Knowledge, which you receive direct from the Holy Spirit, may cover an infinite number of things in your daily life. The "word" can relate to anything; from something trivial such as where you may have misplaced your keys, to providing life-saving knowledge on how to solve an impending crisis or emergency. With our *spiritual knowledge* being so limited, so imperfect, and so incomplete, we all need Words of Knowledge on a regular basis. It is probably the only way that we can make it through life victoriously and to fulfil our divine destinies in God.

How does the Holy Spirit transmit a Word of Knowledge?

Romans 8:16 tells us that, *"The Spirit Himself bears witness with our spirit that we are children of God."* The number one way that the Holy Spirit communicates a Word of Knowledge is through the *'inner witness'*. God's word tells us that the Holy Spirit *"bears witness with our human spirits."* This "knowing" is what is referred to as the **inner witness**. It's when, all of a sudden, we receive an unquestionable type of knowing on the inside of us. We just **know**, *that we know... that we know!*

Whenever the Holy Spirit speaks to our spirit, we do not hear an audible voice. The *voice* of the Spirit transmitting a message to our spirit generates a quiet assurance. It is a peaceful "knowing" about something. The question is, "How can we distinguish the voice of this inner witness? Are there any qualities that we must be able to identify? And what differentiates the inner witness from ordinary thoughts or imagination?"

Here are seven characteristics or qualities we must recognise:

1. **The inner witness is different from human reasoning.** It is not mental knowledge or logical rational.

2. **The inner witness is not a physical feeling.** Since the inner witness is the voice of the Holy Spirit to our spirit, it will bypass our feelings.

3. **The inner witness is best recognised by eliminating other voices.** Make sure it is not the flesh that desires something.

4. **The inner witness is surrounded by peace.** It is an awareness of perfect peace. It is the peace of God that is beyond understanding, reasoning, or human logic.

5. **The inner witness is a strong conviction.** The inner witness makes us absolutely certain about what the Lord is saying.

6. **The inner witness is very distinctive.** The voice of the Holy Spirit, speaking to our heart, is as distinctive as any other voice.

7. **The inner witness is persistent when necessary.** The voice of the Holy Spirit will keep prompting us until we respond.

Why Inner Knowledge?

Colossians 1:9 says, *"For this cause we also, since the day we heard it, do not cease to pray for you, and to desire that you might be **filled with the knowledge of His will** in all wisdom and spiritual understanding."* The Greek word for knowledge is "epignosis" (ἐπίγνωσις), which means *detailed, exact, complete, full knowledge.* Natural knowledge is fallible. It comes from the five senses, and therefore, it works from the outside in. But the knowledge we are talking about is created, transmitted and received entirely on the inside. That way, 'knowledge' from the Holy Spirit is exact and complete.

The Holy Spirit transmits "knowledge" from Himself to our spirit without error or inaccuracy. Our spirit is a safe guide because we are a *new creation* in Christ Jesus. God has all areas covered because He does not want His *gifts* to be tainted by human error. Notice that "knowledge" from God is perfect and complete, therefore, there is never anything wrong with the transmission. It is the hearer only, who can misinterpret or misunderstand. How many times did Jesus say, *"He who has ears, let him hear."* The Lord was telling people to pay careful attention to what He is saying so that they don't misunderstand Him. However, when the Holy Spirit came, all that was able to change.

Now, God's Spirit speaks directly with our spirit (on the inside of us) and our spiritual ears can hear *perfectly* - provided they know who they should be listening to.

The devil will always try to use the cares of this world to draw our attention away from the *voice* of God. This seriously impedes our ability to hear! A *care*, is an overwhelming mental concern, worry, or anguish. What brings about care is listening to, and then meditating on, the devil's lies. Cares amplify the devil's voice. Five times in the sixth chapter of Matthew's gospel (Matthew 6:25, 6:27, 6:38, 6:31, 6:34), Jesus admonishes us not to take on the cares of the world – the anxieties of this life. What exactly is Jesus telling us? *"Don't switch off your receiver, for at any moment, the Holy Spirit can* **transmit** *what you need to hear."*

Indeed, *"Seek first the kingdom of God, and His righteousness; and* **all these things** *will be added"* (Matthew 6:33). Seeking first the kingdom of God is simply prioritising and placing the things of the Spirit **first**. Which is, making sure you are in a position to hear the voice of God and receive "knowledge" from His Spirit at all times. Are you positioned to receive what God's Spirit intends for you? Or are you ignorant of spiritual matters?

5

The Gift of Faith

In 1 Corinthians 12:9 the apostle Paul is talking about the diversities of the Gifts of the Holy Spirit and the various manifestations of the Spirit, and he declares, *"To another **faith** by the same Spirit."* This is the gift or the manifestation of faith. However, there are different kinds of faith. The most prominent is 'healing faith'. In Luke 8:42-48, Jesus was on His way to the house of Jairus, whose daughter had just died. As the crowd followed Him, pushing and shoving Him along and trying to get close, suddenly Jesus stopped. He said, *"Who touched Me?"* Peter's response was, *"Lord, You must be kidding! Everybody is pushing and shoving You. Everyone within ten yards has touched You."* Yet Jesus said, *"No, I felt power go out of Me."* So a woman came and knelt before Him. Trembling, she confessed! For the past twelve years this woman had been haemorrhaging. We are told that she had spent all of her money on doctors and was not restored.

However, this woman believed that if she could just touch the hem of His garment, she would receive her miracle. So, she made her way through the crowd, most probably on her knees in dusty dirty conditions, until she got close enough to touch the hem of the Lord's garment.

Immediately her haemorrhaging ceased. She was totally healed! Jesus then looks at her and says, *"Daughter, be of good cheer because your faith has made you whole."* This could be classified as healing faith. However, in order to do what she had just done, this woman must have possessed another kind of faith. She must have received a supernatural boldness directly from the Holy Spirit – *"gift of faith."*

Let me explain... In that culture, a woman was deemed impure for seven days from the beginning of her menstrual flow (Leviticus 12:2; 15:19). Anyone who touches a woman during that time becomes unclean until the evening (Leviticus 15:19). Whoever touches her bed or anything she sits on during the week is unclean until evening and must wash his/her clothes and bathe with water (verses 20-23). Women were kept separate from the local community during their menstrual cycle. Hence, this woman must have been treated far worse!

Anyone who knew about her illness would avoid her at all cost. She couldn't go about in society and mingle in the marketplace with the other women, since a touch from her would make someone unclean. She couldn't attend ceremonial occasions or synagogue worship. So, she resorts to secrecy. She probably wasn't known in Capernaum. She must have come incognito - her condition carefully concealed, but she has **fortitude**. Imagine the embarrassment if she were caught or even noticed. This woman would have been ostracised and publicly humiliated. Yet, somehow she had the boldness and strength to go out into a large crowd of people to find (and touch) Jesus – undetected!

Due to the positioning of the hem on the cloak, I am convinced that this woman must have crawled on her hands and knees in order to touch the Lord's hem. What determination she must have displayed!

The cloak - the Tallith or Goltha - was a square garment that bore

The cloak - the Tallith or Goltha - was a square garment that bore tassels at the corners in fulfilment of the commands in Numbers 15:38-39 and Deuteronomy 22:12 as a reminder to obey the laws of the Lord. The strands that made up the tassel probably included at least one of hyacinth (light violet to moderate purple) colour and several strands of white. In Luke 8:44 the outer clothing is expressed by the Greek word *'himation'*, a cloak or robe. Therefore, the hem must have been quite low to the ground, and the woman would not be able to touch it standing up. Remember, the crowd was tightly packed around the Lord, and no way could she have got close to Him and then bent down! She was definitely on the ground already!

The *gift* of **faith** that healed this woman is evident, for Jesus Himself commends her for having the faith to draw healing from Him. He even calls her daughter! Yet, what about the *faith* that got her there? How was she able to overcome immeasurable obstacles in order to touch the hem of His cloak? This is another kind of faith. To accomplish what is normally impossible, she had a *gift of faith*. It was just as miraculous as the healing this woman received because I believe it was totally Holy Spirit inspired. We can all learn from this story since it may take another kind of faith to get us to the place where we can receive our miracle.

In Matthew 15:21-28 we find another woman who wasn't ready to allow tradition to prevent her from receiving a miracle. She was a gentile from the area of Tyre and she came to Jesus concerning her daughter, who was severely demon possessed. When the disciples came and said, *"Lord do something. She is troubling us."* To them He said, *"I am not sent but to the lost sheep of the house of Israel."* So, she then came directly to Jesus. *"Lord, help me."* And He said, *"It is not right to take the children's bread and to throw it to the little puppies."*

"True, Lord, but the little puppies," she said, *"eat the crumbs that fall from the master's table."* Then, Jesus answered and said to her, *"O woman, **great** is your **faith**! Let it be to you as you desire."* Her daughter was healed from that very hour. The miracle was released by another kind of faith, and that is what brought healing to her

daughter. Such supernatural boldness and tenacity is a mark of the Gift of Faith.

Mark 10:46-52 tells us, *"Now they came to Jericho. As He went out of Jericho with His disciples and a great multitude, blind Bartimaeus, the son of Timaeus, sat by the road begging. And when he heard that it was Jesus of Nazareth, he began to cry out and say, "Jesus, Son of David, have mercy on me!" Then many warned him to be quiet; but he cried out all the more, "Son of David, have mercy on me!" So Jesus stood still and commanded him to be called. Then they called the blind man, saying to him, "Be of good cheer. Rise, He is calling you." And throwing aside his garment, he rose and came to Jesus. So Jesus answered and said to him, "What do you want Me to do for you?" The blind man said to Him, "Rabboni, that I may receive my sight." Then Jesus said to him, "Go your way; your faith has made you well." And immediately he received his sight and followed Jesus on the road."* A blind man receiving His sight is a miracle! Yet, why did Jesus stop? Yes, the Lord responds to the cries of His people, but there was something else that compelled him to stop.

We have just heard that many people warned Bartimaeus to be quiet, but he cried out even louder! Let me ask you... Can a blind man see where a person is when there is so much noise and activity going on? No! So, what made this man so insistent and bold? Again, I believe he was *faith* inspired by the Holy Spirit. It was the Gift of Faith preparing him for his miracle. Bartimaeus had no doubt that his miracle was near, and he wasn't going to let anything or anyone steal it!

From these accounts, it would seem that the Gift of Faith is related directly to healings or miracles. In fact, in the listing of the manifestations of the Spirit, I do not think it is accidental that the Gift of Faith precedes the Gifts of Healings. Here is a very interesting fact, the word "faith" is only mentioned twice in the Old Testament and once in a very negative way. However, it is mentioned 247 times in the New Testament. Deuteronomy 32:20 and Habakkuk 2:4, are the only two mentions of *faith* in the Old Testament. Why is that? I am sure it has to do with the Holy Spirit.

"So then faith comes by hearing, and hearing by the (spoken) word of God" (Romans 10:17). Faith, the Bible says, comes by hearing and hearing by the Word of God. It does not say, *"Faith comes by reading,"* or, *"Faith comes by hearing a preacher."* Faith comes by hearing God. God speaks **faith** to our hearts, and the Holy Spirit, the third person of the Godhead, is the designated speaker. He is the Person who speaks the Word to our hearts and causes **faith** to come alive. The Holy Spirit dwells inside of all believers - to lead us and to speak to us. It is the great promise of the Father. However, this was not possible in the Old Testament. *"I am telling you the truth: It's good for you that I'm going away. If I don't go away, the Helper won't come to you. If I go, I'll send him to you"* (John 16:7).

Jesus said He did not speak on *"His own initiative,"* but rather, spoke only what the Father told Him to say (John 12:49). Now, Jesus says that the Holy Spirit will not speak on His own initiative but will take the words of Jesus and speak them to us. Hence, we are to speak only what the Holy Spirit speaks to us. In John 16:12-15, we find Jesus divulging information to us through the voice of the Holy Spirit. I believe this is referring to the speaking (communication) of **faith** to the heart of man (as mentioned in Romans 10:17).

A "word" from the Holy Spirit is what brings substance and reality to our hopes and ultimately makes them visible. It is a **faith** creator! The Old Testament saints could have none of this! The Gift of Faith is reserved for those who have received a risen Christ. Those who have received the *gift* of the Holy Spirit!

In Acts 3:6-9, Peter was going into the temple with John at the hour of prayer, around three o'clock in the afternoon. There was a man about forty years old who had never walked in his entire life. He was begging for money from the people going into the temple to worship. Peter said to the man, *"Look over here"* and the man turned, expecting to receive some money. Then Peter said, *"Silver and gold I do not have, but what I do have I give you: In the name of Jesus Christ of Nazareth, rise up and walk." And he took him by the right hand and lifted him up, and immediately his feet and ankle bones received strength. So he, leaping up, stood and walked and entered the temple with them - walking, leaping, and praising God. And all the people saw him walking and praising God.*

Then, as Peter explained the miracle in Acts 3:16, he said, *"And His name, that is Jesus, through faith in His name has made this man strong whom you see and you know."* It was *through the name of Jesus and faith in the name of Jesus* that this man was now standing there healed of that infirmity of over forty years. But then he went on to say, *"Yes, the faith which is by Him."* In other words, Peter is not saying it is my great faith, but he is acknowledging that it was the **faith** received directly from Jesus. This was the Gift of Faith in operation. It was *extraordinary* faith that caused Peter to say to the man, *"What I have I give to you. In the name of Jesus Christ of Nazareth, stand up and walk!"* Peter is saying, it was *faith* that is *by* Him (recognising this was the Gift of Faith in operation), which brought about healing and the miracle for this man.

Notice, here we see three gifts in operation: *the Gift of Faith, the Gift of Healings, and the Gift of the Working of Miracles.*

In Acts 6:8 we read, *"And Stephen full of **faith** and power did great wonders and miracles among the people."* The miracles and wonders were attributed to the fact that he was *filled* with faith. In Acts 14, when Paul was in Lystra preaching, there was again a lame man who had never walked and Paul perceived that this man had the *faith* to be healed. The man was probably very intent in listening to Paul, so he said with a loud voice, *"Stand up straight on your feet!"* And he leaped and walked. Again, this is probably the Gift of Faith, declaring to this man the "word of faith." ...*Jesus of Nazareth, makes you whole.*

I remember when my mother-in-law, Mary, had flown over to visit us in South Africa and unfortunately she pulled her back out on the first day. Mary had travelled a long way and was now very likely to spend many days (even weeks) incapacitated. I thought to myself, "This is not right! God needs to do something." At that very moment, I felt an urgency in my spirit to go and pray for her. Now, picture this... Mary was in bed unable to move. She was in pain and looking very fragile. When all of a sudden, I walk into the bedroom, determined to pray and lay my hands on her. Not what she was expecting – I'm sure! But God had another plan, a far better plan. As I approached the bed, extraordinary boldness came upon me. Before we could even engage in conversation, I grabbed her by the hand, pulled her out of bed, and started to dance with her. The moment her feet hit the ground, she was healed! We started to shout and began to dance freely, praising God and thanking Him for His miracle-working power. It was a while before I realised the full extent of what had just happened. Imagine if I had missed God! What if I dragged Mary out of bed and injured her back even more! Yet, the Gift of Faith was in operation, and I could not help myself.

The Holy Spirit had compelled me to do exactly what He was intending, praise God for that! Mary was able to enjoy her time in the sun without pain or discomfort.

Many times, when I am praying for the sick, the Gift of Faith suddenly comes upon me. Often it is with people that can't walk or have intense pain when walking. Most of the time, I do what I did with Mary. I grab them by the hand and get them to do something spontaneous! Every time, the power of God is released and they start walking freely (even running) without pain. Recently, an elderly lady came out for prayer carrying a walking stick. I could see she was in much discomfort. The Lord gave me a Word of Knowledge that it was her right hip. So, I told her to put down her walking stick and take my arm. As we started to walk the pain in her hip left and she started to run. I can't tell you how many times this has happened!

As pastor of a church, it is important that I respond quickly to the prompting of God's Spirit. Many times He will ask me to do what in the natural seems extreme or foolish. However, I have learnt that obeying God's voice is the very means He uses to bring about astonishing results. At a service recently, I asked a man with damaged vertebra in his back to start jumping and God was able to start a healing that was otherwise impossible. At our New Year service, I gave instructions for the congregation to walk around the sanctuary 7 times... we experienced many miracles!

God, according to His sovereign purposes and at various times, does manifest His supreme power and His limitless ability. Those times of divine expression are always thrilling and exciting. Therefore, let us remain open to what He intends to do. He is the Almighty and shall manifest Himself in whichever way He desires. Let us not have closed minds, and let us not relegate God's ability (to intervene) to some special service or event.

Rather, let us realise that Jesus Christ is the same yesterday, today and forever. He can sovereignly manifest His divine power to perform *miracles, signs* and *wonders* today. Therefore, let us rejoice and give Him all the glory whenever He does!

Remember... The **Gift of Faith** is often accompanied by great "works of faith." The Holy Spirit distributes this *gift* to certain believers in order to encourage and build up the Church and its confidence in God. Those who are used with the Gift of Faith have complete trust in the sovereignty of God. They take Him at His Word and fully depend on Him in every situation. In fact, they always *expect* God to move and are not surprised when He performs a miracle. Such people know how to draw upon the 'River of Life' by means of the *spiritual gifts*.

As with the Word of Wisdom, which is needed to **apply** the other gifts, the Gift of Faith is often needed to **implement** the other gifts. For instance, when either the Gift of Healings or the gift of the Working of Miracles is needed, the Gift of Faith will be there to *implement* which ever *gift* is necessary. Note, we require a 'special kind of faith' to unreservedly pronounce certain things, and we require a 'supernatural faith' when we are directed to do something distinctive for somebody to receive a miracle. On several occasions, it was necessary for me to *"say or do"* things that were totally out of my comfort zone. Yet, because I was compelled by God's Spirit to do them, I couldn't resist!

One day, when I was praying for the sick at the end of a service, I saw a woman standing in the prayer-line who was visiting the church for the very first time. As I approached her, the Holy Spirit prompted me to declare "loudly" that her husband would live and not die. Now, I knew nothing about this woman! Yet, God wanted to do something miraculous and needed my voice to declare it.

As it transpired, the man who was terminally ill in hospital and had been given only two days to live, was our resident atheist. In sheer desperation, his wife came to the church to asked for help. I wasn't sure if she even believed in God. Her husband, on the other hand, would regularly come to our services because he liked the atmosphere and the inspiring way I did "my talks." Nevertheless, once I had declared that he would live and not die, she started to cry profusely, and later she gave her heart to Jesus. Yet, that was only the beginning!

Over the next 48 hours, her husband's condition got increasingly better. Instead of dying in two days, his vital organs recovered fully and he was let out of hospital in just two weeks. To the amazement of all the doctors! Of course, he then came back to our church and gave his heart to Jesus and started to faithfully serve the Lord. Yet, it took an act of **faith** to declare openly that he would live and not die! Thereafter, God was able to perform the miracle that was needed to restore this man to perfect health. It was a testimony that impacted on many people's lives.

Notice, how God answered the prayers of an atheist's wife, who probably never prayed correctly. God's love has no boundaries! It's the religious attitudes found in the modern-day church that restrict and impede God's love! All the *gifts* of the Holy Spirit are discharged from the unconditional love of God. *"And now abide faith, hope, love, these three; but the greatest of these is love"* (1 Corinthians 13:13). Before God moves, the Church must first be moved with compassion. Hence, the love of God **precedes** any operation of the Gifts of the Holy Spirit. So, if you sincerely desire to be used by God in this capacity, you must first allow the love of God to flow "in" and "through" you. His amazing love never, ever fails (1 Corinthians 13:8).

Why is the Gift of Faith Necessary Today?

The Gift of Faith is necessary today for the same reasons the gift was indispensable when the Church was birthed:

- **It is one of the best gifts** (1 Corinthians 12:31). Faith may be less spectacular than Miracles, but faith is probably a superior *gift* than Working of Miracles. Jesus Himself talked about *"an evil and adulterous generation that seeks after a sign"* (Matthew 12:39). The Gift of Faith trusts God through the trial without any great show of power. It is far better to have faith in the storm than to cry out for a miraculous intervention. The world admires great miracles but the Lord loves to see faith.

- **It makes the impossible possible.** The Gift of Faith is able to believe for the impossible because it sees beyond the natural (it sees the unseen). When Jesus heard that Lazarus was sick, He said *"This sickness is not unto death, but for the glory of God, that the Son of God might be glorified"*, and then he waited. (John 11:4-6). He knew Lazarus had died, but He also knew Lazarus would be raised from the dead. Jesus never had any doubt! As with us, faith is what pleases the Father!

- **It produces unstoppable / undeniable determination.** This 'special kind of faith' – a supernatural empowerment of faith, produces boldness to stand against all of God's enemies, and makes us *more than conquerors* in spiritual warfare. The Church is under attack and we need this kind of determination and holy-boldness to permeate through our congregations!

- **It enables ordinary people do extra-ordinary things.** God is waiting for His Church to step into the fullness of what He has predestined for these times. He wants to use ordinary people to accomplish impossible tasks for the extension of His kingdom here on earth. *"I will build My church, and the gates of hell will not prevail against it"* (Matthew 16:18)

*"God, who at various times and in various ways **spoke** in time past to the fathers by the prophets, has in these last days **spoken** to us by His Son, whom He has appointed heir of all things, through whom also He made the worlds; who being the brightness of His glory and the express image of His person, and upholding all things by the **word of His power**, when He had by Himself purged our sins, sat down at the right hand of the Majesty on high, having become so much better than the angels, as He has by inheritance obtained a more excellent name than they" (Hebrews 1:1-4)*

6

The Gifts of Healings

*How God anointed Jesus of Nazareth with the Holy Spirit and power, and how He went around doing good and **healing all who were under the power of the devil**, because God was with Him.*

(Acts 10:38)

The first thing I would like to mention concerning the Gifts of Healings is that there are various kinds of gifts and different kinds of healings. Isn't it interesting that the literal phrase in *verse 9* is not "gift of healing" but "gifts of healings" - two plurals! The Holy Spirit will manifest the exact gift you need to get healed and in the precise way you need to get healed. We don't all get healed the same way or in the same fashion. It is *as He wills, when He wills,* and *the way He wills.* This would suggest that no one person has a monopoly on any manner of healings that may be necessary. Paul's own experience teaches us that there are *varied* Gifts of Healings that can be given to us at different times and for diverse illnesses. However, there are no guarantees! Just because we have received a *gift* to heal in the past, doesn't mean we will receive a similar *gift* on any particular occasion in the future.

1 Corinthians 12:11 says, *"it is the Spirit who apportions the gifts to each one individually as He pleases."* God is sovereign, therefore, He dispenses *spiritual gifts* whenever He chooses and to whomever He wishes. We can't manipulate the operation of the Gifts of the Holy Spirit. I would also like to point out that they are not for self-exaltation or self-promotion. The gifts are meant to be expressions of love. Paul says in 1 Corinthians 13:2, *"Though I have all faith so as to remove mountains, but have not love, I am nothing."* Gifts are not the main thing... **Love** is the main thing. Spiritual gifts are channels through which to love others and express true love. 1 Corinthians 14:1 says, *"Make love your aim, and earnestly desire the spiritual gifts..."* Once you have set your heart to pursue love, you place yourself in a position to be zealous for *spiritual gifts*. Among those spiritual gifts are the Gifts of Healings.

Throughout biblical history, God has manifested His power to heal. Genesis 17, documents the healing of Abimelech, his wife, and his maid servants in answer to Abraham's prayer. We know that God gave wonderful promises of healing to the children of Israel. Again in the Old Testament we find that Miriam, the sister of Moses, was healed of leprosy in answer to the prayers of Moses. Hezekiah was actually healed on his deathbed as the result of prayer. Later, as we look at the ministry of Jesus, there can be no denying that "healing the sick" was one of the predominant facets of the Lord's ministry. When Jesus sent the disciples out, He gave them instructions to go into every town and preach the kingdom, and to **heal** the sick! Therefore, healing the sick was not only a dominant factor of the ministry of Christ but also of the disciples (His followers).

Note, the Bible never talks about the gift of healers - men who themselves possess the gift of healing. It is clearly the *gifts*, plural, of *healings*, plural – of the Holy Spirit.

On many occasions, as the Lord has touched my body, I have personally received *supernatural* healing. Furthermore, as I have ministered to the sick, through the laying on of hands, I have seen God do *exceedingly, abundantly above all that I can ask, think or imagine, according to the power that works in us* (Ephesians 3:20).

The number of people healed, and the various kinds of *healings* that I've witnessed over the years, are too plentiful to mention. Additionally, I firmly believe that the supernatural power to exercise healing (of any kind) is though the correct use of the Name of Jesus.

Due to the fact that sickness and disease come directly from the devil, and not God, the Gifts of Healings must be executed with authority. In Acts 10:38, it tells us distinctly that Jesus went about doing good and healing all who were **under the control** of the devil (literal Greek). Therefore, the devil uses sickness and disease to *control* people. The only way these people can be set free from this evil oppression, is for a believer to exercise *authority* over that condition. I'm talking about the *authority* that Jesus handed over to His Church – the *authority in His Name.*

Why is it necessary for us to use the name of Jesus Christ when performing spiritual acts of service (like healing the sick)? Is there some specific revelation concerning the name that needs to be obtained in order to have our prayers or requests to the Father granted? And is this revelation necessary to access the power of the Holy Spirit? The answers to these questions are very important because the answers have a direct impact on our ability to perform various spiritual deeds of power. When we were elevated "together" with Christ, we were also given certain responsibilities that accompany this high position of *authority*. One of these responsibilities is to *heal the sick* and set free all who are *oppressed* of the devil.

The practical definition of the word *'name'* in both the Hebrew and the Greek languages denotes a mark, or the identification of a person or thing. However, many times the *'name'* of an individual mentioned in God's word is used to express that person's *authority*, character, or reputation. It is also well known in biblical and rabbinical teachings that the phrase *'in the name of'* is used to connect the person having authority, to the one from whom the authority comes.

Hence, uttering the phrase *'in the name of Jesus Christ'* has no power or meaning in and of itself. More importantly, these words have no real power over anything nor do they have the ability to cause anything to occur in the physical or spiritual realms unless the person who uses these words is authorised to use the *authority* and power that resides with God the Father in Christ Jesus. To speak *in the name of Jesus Christ* is to take His consent, as the Lord's representative, and speak on His behalf. Many believers just say the words *'in the name of Jesus Christ'* without understanding what they are intended to mean or invoke. Yet, it is another thing entirely to truly understand the *authority* behind these words. For when they are spoken by one who has been duly authorised by God to use the resurrection power of the Holy Spirit, incredible things happen.

The *"name"* of Jesus Christ describes and represents the highest ranking position in the universe - King of Kings and Lord of Lords! Philippians 2:9-11,

> *Therefore God also has highly exalted Him and given Him the name which is above every name, that at the name of Jesus every knee should bow, of those in heaven, and of those on earth, and of those under the earth, and that every tongue should confess that Jesus Christ is Lord, to the glory of God the Father.*

When the apostles, and others of the early church spoke, they clearly described who they were speaking about and by whose *authority* they were performing miracles.

So much so that they were even warned not to speak or teach in "that Name!" Acts 4:18, *"So they called them and commanded them not to speak at all nor teach in the name of Jesus."* When we speak, we should also make a clear distinction between our God and the gods of this world. This fundamental truth must be emphasised when representing God the Father or performing any supernatural deeds on His behalf. The Bible clearly shows that all existing authority and power resides in God the Father. It's through His *authority* and power that all things (and beings), whether physical or spiritual, are able to exist and exert physical or spiritual action and influence. Paul declares, *"Let every soul be subject to higher authorities, for there is no authority except from God; but the authorities that exist have been ordained by God "* (Romans 13:1).

The truth is, all authority has been passed on to the Church, (Matthew 28:18-19) and this authority is activated only when we use the 'name of Jesus Christ' . The early church new exactly what it meant to use that wonderful Name. In Acts 3:6 we see why everyone was so upset... Then Peter said, *"Silver and gold I do not have, but what I do have I give you: In the name of Jesus Christ of Nazareth, rise up and walk."* When Peter used the Name, he got miraculous results! This put fear into the rulers and religious people of his day. *"So that it spreads no further among the people, let us severely threaten them, that from now on they speak to no man in this name"* (Acts 4:17).

More so, the Lord's name has authority in three worlds! *"That at the name of Jesus every knee should bow, of those in heaven, and of those on earth, and of those under the earth"* (Philippians 2:10). We must therefore, apply Jesus' authority over any sickness or disease that has a name. Why? Because whatever condition it is, it must bow its knee. Yes, *in the name of Jesus Christ*, sickness and disease must leave (Acts 3:1-8).

Yet, we need to have true **faith** in that Name. We 'stand in' for Jesus when we command healing to take place. Yes, we have authority over all the works of the devil through that Name, and, remember this, the power and authority in using the name of Jesus Christ is not in the actual use of the words. They are not some magical words in and of themselves. The awesome power demonstrated in the *'name of Jesus Christ'* is caused by the actual power and authority of Jesus Christ Himself.

E W Kenyan said, *"The degree to which you use the name of Jesus, is the degree to which the forces of darkness will obey you."* The Name of Jesus was given to the Church 'to use'. Every mention in scripture of the use of the Name is in direct reference to the Body of Christ. The Name of Jesus legally belongs to the church (His bride). The wonderful name of Jesus has total authority in three realms – in heaven, on Earth and under the Earth (in the spiritual and physical realms, and even over dark spiritual forces). It's just as powerful and as effective in whatever dimension it is being proclaimed. The early church knew this, and they prayed accordingly.

Acts 4:30, *"By stretching out Your hand to heal, and that signs and wonders may be done through the name of Your holy Servant Jesus."*

When using the name of Jesus, we should be confident that sickness will leave! We must understand fully the authority it has over **all** the works of the devil. *"For this purpose the Son of God was manifested, that He might destroy the works of the devil"* (1 John 3:8). Because of the *authority* we have received, healing is for today! Also, the Gifts of Healings help to fulfil the promises God has given us concerning wholeness and soundness. God wants His children to be blessed with good health. *"But He was wounded for our transgressions, He was bruised for our iniquities; The chastisement for our peace was upon Him, And by His stripes we are healed"* (Isaiah 53:5).

Another spiritual principle we need to fully comprehend, when operating in any of the Gifts of the Holy Spirit, is the importance of "the Anointing." In Luke 4:18, when announcing His ministry and mission, the Lord Jesus quoted from Isaiah 53 and declared,

> *The Spirit of the Lord is upon Me because He has **anointed** Me to preach the gospel to the poor; He has sent Me to heal the broken-hearted; to proclaim liberty to the captives, and recovery of sight to the blind, to set at liberty those who are oppressed.*

The Spirit of the Lord and the Anointing are synonymous with each other. When the Holy Spirit is active so too is the Anointing!

In the Old testament, three types of people were anointed. First was the anointing of the priests. Leviticus 8:12, *"And he poured of the anointing oil upon Aaron's head, and anointed him, to sanctify him."* It is noteworthy that this anointing took place only one time for each priest. Second, there was the anointing of the kings. I Samuel 16:13, *"Then Samuel took the horn of oil, and anointed him in the midst of his brethren: and the Spirit of the Lord came upon David from that day forward. So Samuel rose up, and went to Ramah."* Likewise, this anointing was a one-time ritual. Third, there was the anointing of the prophets. I Kings 19:16, *"Also you shall anoint Jehu the son of Nimshi as king over Israel. And Elisha the son of Shaphat of Abel*

Meholah you shall anoint as prophet in your place." Again, it took place only one time, for each prophet.

Since our Lord Jesus was a high priest, king and prophet, He was anointed for all three offices. Luke 4:18,

> *The Spirit of the Lord is upon Me, because He has **anointed** me to preach the Gospel to the poor; He has sent Me to heal the broken-hearted, to preach deliverance to the captives, and recovering of sight to the blind, to set at liberty those who are oppressed.*

Acts 4:27, *"For truly against Your holy Servant Jesus, whom You **anointed**... were all these gathered together."*

Acts 10:38, *"How God **anointed** Jesus of Nazareth with the Holy Ghost and with power: Who went about doing good, and healing all that were oppressed of the Devil; for God was with Him."*

We must remember, even though Jesus had the Spirit without measure, He was **anointed** in a different way. For the Holy Spirit had not yet been sent (as per the Lord's promise in John 14:16). Everything changed when the Holy Spirit came permanently on the Day of Pentecost - to empower and equip the Church. Before that day, a select number of people would be "anointed" for a specific task, office or purpose. Now, the anointing, in the form of the Holy Spirit, is residing in all believers. The anointing is now a Person! God's Spirit is the Anointing! The Anointing is with us right now, to manifest His Gifts. Unless we understand this principle, we will always be waiting for the Holy Spirit to do something. When in fact, He already intends to do exactly what Jesus would do if He was present!

All believers are "called" to walk in the same miracle-working power Jesus demonstrated. Unfortunately, the word *anointing* today has acquired a general meaning in the Church. It is used to denote an all-purpose type of blessing. Scripturally, however, there is no such thing as *an anointing*, only **the Anointing** - the anointing of the Holy Spirit. As mentioned, in the Old Testament all who served God had to be anointed. This has been replaced in the New Testament by the blessed Holy Spirit. Now, all of us receive the same Holy Spirit for our work of service. Before the day of Pentecost, Hebrew priests were anointed and carried the fragrance of the oil with them, but since Pentecost, believers instead carry the beautiful aroma of the "Spirit of Christ." As Christians, our anointing flows out of Christ's anointing, and we receive it only from Him: *"Of His fullness we have all received"* (John 1:16). Therefore, "anointings" are not to be expected every time we meet a special evangelist or preacher.

Today, the **Anointing** is for all believers, for all are called to serve. It is absolutely essential we understand that the Holy Spirit is "He",and not "it." The Spirit is not an impersonal force, a sort of spiritual electricity. The anointing of God is not just power or *gifts* but the Person of the Holy Spirit. When Jesus healed the sick, it was because He was anointed with the Holy Spirit!

The Anointing renews us; we do not renew it. The Holy Spirit is the Spirit of newness and freshness. 1 John 2:27 says: *"The anointing which you have received from Him abides in you."* If we are doing the work God called us to, then the Anointing rests upon us without ever decreasing. We receive it like a waterfall fed by a never-failing river. All that's required of us is to release His powers by working in **His name** – letting the rivers of living water flow. The inward Spirit is always seen by outward results, through the manifestation of the Gifts of the Holy Spirit. Never forget that the power of God occurs only with the Holy Spirit, who reveals the beauty of Jesus - the Anointed One - and His never-failing love.

Yet another principle to understand when operating in the gifts of healings is that **healing** is a by-product of the stripes Jesus endured before dying on the cross:

*"But He was wounded for our transgressions, he was bruised for our iniquities; the chastisement for our peace was upon Him, and **by His stripes we are healed**"* (Isaiah 53:5);

"They brought to Him many who were demon-possessed. And He cast out the spirits with a word, and healed all who were sick, that it might be fulfilled which was spoken by Isaiah the prophet, saying: 'He Himself took our infirmities and bore our sicknesses'" (Matt. 8:16-17);

*"Who Himself bore our sins in His own body on the tree, that we, having died to sins might live for righteousness - **by whose stripes you were healed"** (1 Pet. 2:24).

There is a vital connection between us and the healing ministry of Jesus. We are His Body on earth today (1 Corinthians 3:16), and, through God's Spirit, we carry on His ministry. Therefore, all believers should display the same passion for healing that Jesus exhibited. The Bible mentions numerous reasons why Jesus healed:

- to restore human life;
- to deliver people from demons;
- to reveal God (and God's heart).

As His body on earth today, we have a duty to release His healing power to our generation. They all need to encounter the power and authority of God and experience the Gifts of the Holy Spirit first hand. If we don't do this, their lives will be void of God's presence and power. Here are seven ways the Body of Christ can release God's healing power today (some of which have already been mentioned):

1. **Through demonstration of the Gifts of Healings.** There are times when God releases the Gifts of Healings, and in some instances, the anointing is so great that even clothes can be used as a point of contact. *"Now God worked unusual miracles by the hands of Paul, so that even handkerchiefs or aprons were brought from his body to the sick, and the diseases left them and the evil spirits went out of them"* (Acts 19:11-12). Note, people are always healed in a 'Spirit-saturated' environment, where the Gifts of Healings are unrestricted.

2. **Through the laying on of hands.** It is the freedom of every true believer to lay hands on the sick and pray for their recovery. When this is done, a spiritual transferral takes place in the invisible realm of the spirit. *"They will take up serpents; and if they drink anything deadly, it will by no means hurt them; they will lay hands on the sick, and they will recover"* (Mark 16:18).

3. **Through the elders, prayer and anointing oil.** Here the sick person, by his own choice, calls for the pastors/elders to pray over him. Confession of sin and heart preparation is also needed. The oil symbolizes the work of the Holy Spirit. *"Is anyone among you sick? Let him call for the elders of the church, and let them pray over him, anointing him with oil in the name of the Lord"* (James 5:14).

4. **Through speaking the Word in faith.** In the following verse, we can see that a believer must clearly announce his need — he/she must speak it out. And this word must be spoken with confidence. Confession is a wonderful tool for us to use, and keep using, until the sickness leaves! *"For assuredly, I say to you, whoever says to this mountain, 'Be removed and be cast into the sea,' and does not doubt in his heart, but believes that those things he says will be done, he will have whatever he says"* (Mark 11:23). We can also "send" the Word to heal, as the centurion requested Jesus to do in Matthew 8:8, *The centurion answered and said, "Lord, I am not worthy that You should come under my roof. But only speak a word, and my servant will be healed."* Psalm 107:20 confirms this spiritual process, *"He sent His word and healed them, and delivered them from their ruins."*

5. **Through the power of agreement.** One of the reasons God gave us the "church family" was for us to learn the power of agreement. In Psalm 133, the writer speaks of God's commanded blessing when two or more get into agreement about the will of God. When the local church comes into agreement concerning healing, it's extremely powerful! *"Again I say to you that if two of you agree on earth concerning anything that they ask, it will be done for them by My Father in heaven. For where two or three are gathered together in My name, I am there in the midst of them"* (Matt. 18:19-20).

6. **Through exercising our own faith.** Our personal 'faith-saturated' prayers deliver us from sickness and disease. Healing from all our ailments is possible! Real faith will move

on with life, in spite of any setbacks. It is a "God said it and that settles it" attitude! *"Therefore I say to you, whatever things you ask when you pray, believe that you receive them, and you will have them"* (Mark 11:24).

7. **Through the Name of Jesus.** As mentioned in detail earlier, the name of Jesus is a powerful force against disease and all evil forces. *"And whatever you ask in My name, that I will do, that the Father may be glorified in the Son. If you ask anything in My name, I will do it"* (John 14:13-14).

In conclusion, the Gifts of Healings declare the unquestionable character of God. Throughout church history we find believers not only expecting God to do miracles but also experiencing divine healing on a regular basis. The message of the Gospel is... *"that God so loved the world"* (John 3:16), and the *good news* is backed up by tangible evidence of God intervening miraculously in people's lives. Most often, when we least expect it!

I had an experience with the Gifts of Healings that I will never forget... I woke up one Sunday morning, before going to church to preach, feeling very disorientated and sick. In fact, I couldn't see properly – everything was a blur! My mind was telling me to call the doctor or go straight to the hospital emergency. But my spirit was saying, "you are planning to teach on divine health, so why would you not go to church?" As a result, I told my wife Loraine to drive me to church, in spite of my symptoms. So, off we went! All the way to church I was wondering whether I had done the right thing. My symptoms weren't getting any better. If anything, they were probably getting a lot worse! Nevertheless, the moment we arrived I asked the other pastors to pray for me.

During the worship my condition seemed to deteriorate and I began sweating profusely. I also couldn't see my notes or read the Bible. So, I decided to teach about divine health from memory but intended to keep it short. Once I had started, I immediately sensed the Holy Spirit saying to me "pray for the sick." I thought that was a big ask, knowing my condition. Yet, He was persistent so I wasn't able to back off! By now, I was fully committed and completely surrendered to the Lord. I didn't know what to expect, only that He had told me to do it. So, whatever happened was entirely up to Him. After a short message on divine health, I cautiously called people forward who needed a healing touch from God. Note, exercising such restraint was very unlike me because I am usually bold and passionate about the things of the Spirit.

About twenty people came forward for prayer, and I waited to see how I should start ministering to the sick. It is always best to wait and be "led by the Holy Spirit," as He doesn't want us to do things mechanically. I got no instructions, therefore, I decided to begin by praying for the first person standing in line, on my left.

To my amazement, the moment I laid my hands on him I (and not him) was completely healed. All my symptoms left in an instant. I could see clearly, and my strength had returned. I felt great! Consequently, I kept praying for the sick – going down the line one by one. When I had reached the middle of the prayer line, I heard a lady say to me, "Why did you turn up the sound?" Looking straight at her I answered, "I have no control over the sound volume." She then realised that something miraculous had happened. She had been deaf in her left ear for seventeen years and God had just healed her! It had popped open while I was approaching her! We all started to rejoice, praising God for His grace and mercy.

After the service, the woman who received a miraculous touch from God told me exactly what had happened... While I was praying for other people, she looked over and saw a bright light radiating all around me. As this had never happened to her before, she thought that she may be imagining things or be caught up in the moment. After all, the atmosphere was very different and not what she was used to in church. However, as I got closer to her the light got brighter, and that's when everything suddenly got very loud. All she remembers is asking me something about the sound. She then informed me that her husband was a Member of Parliament and that she was not someone prone to exaggeration or strange spiritual experiences.

The amazing thing about this story is that God healed me before I could pray for anyone else, and then proceeded to miraculously restore a woman's deaf ear. Someone who had in fact come forward for back pain! Isn't God amazing? When the Gifts of Healings are in operation, you can expect the unexpected. The Holy Spirit will always do it His way. How exciting - Praise God!

7

The Gift of Working of Miracles

And through the hands of the apostles many signs and wonders were done among the people.

Acts 5:12

The Working of Miracles is an instantaneous activation of divine power that comes upon a believer enabling him/her to accomplish something, which by the laws of nature would be impossible. It's a thoroughly supernatural intervention into the natural order of things. In 1 Corinthians 12:10, it's interesting to observe the two Greek words used: First, "work" ἐνεργήματα translated "working" or "operation" comes from a root word that means *"to display activity, or show oneself operative."* It is where we get the English word energy. Therefore, it's a 'power' word. However, the second word Paul uses is also a power word - δυνάμεων. This word is literally forces (a common military term), so the verse may read, *"yet to another **the operation of forces**."* Observe, when the Holy Spirit manifests the Gift of the Working of Miracles, He is in fact putting into operation the all-powerful all-conquering "forces of heaven!"

A **miracle** is something that is humanly impossible but divinely effortless because it is backed up by all the unseen forces of heaven. When doing anything, the degree of difficulty should always be measured by the capacity of the *'instrument'* that is at work. When God is doing the work, to talk of difficulty would be absurd. Paul the Apostle said to King Agrippa, *"Why should it be thought a thing incredible with you, that God should raise the dead?"* (Acts 26:8). Raising the dead is no problem for God! He breathed life into Adam when he was just an inanimate object made out of mud. God breathed life into Adam (a lifeless object), so why would it be difficult for God to raise the dead?

The Bible is full of miracles, and probably the biggest of these starts in the first verse of Genesis, *"In the beginning God created the heavens and the earth."* Now, if you can believe that, you should not have any trouble with the rest of the Book as it gives you a proper perspective of God. He is wise, omnipotent, and powerful - creating the entire universe by simply saying, "Let there be..." A God who is big enough to do that is big enough to do anything! From the invisible He does the impossible!

Whenever God chooses to release the invisible forces of heaven, the impossible becomes possible, and miracles begin to happen. Many people have difficulty in accepting **miracles**, and that is because they do not truly acknowledge God. They are stuck in the pride of their own intellect. Thinking they already know so much about the world around them. Yet, they only *reason* in the realm of the physical, addressing natural phenomena. They have chosen to exclude the *supernatural* from their thought processes. Therefore, when you talk about a miracle, they are naturally sceptical. They do not believe in a "miracle working" God, so they have to justify their beliefs by rationalising or denying all miraculous or supernatural manifestations.

Miracles are not merely a random display of God's power. Every miracle has a distinct purpose. Think of it this way: *When God works a miracle, He is not just **doing** something - He is also **saying** something!* Often we focus on the astonishing thing that has just happened without considering what message it is intended to convey. Miracles in the Bible never happen without a purpose. When we read a miracle story in the Bible, we ought to be asking ourselves, *"What is God saying through this amazing event?"*

We read of astounding miracles in the time of Moses - as he led the children of Israel out of Egypt. We read of more miracles during the days of Elijah and Elisha. We read of amazing things that happened during the earthly ministry of our Lord Jesus, and we read of other miracles in the book of Acts. However, that's only one side of the story. The other side is that you can read page after page in the Bible without running into any miracles at all. It's not as if miracles were an everyday occurrence (even in the Lord's ministry). They did not happen routinely or predictably. That is, the blind man in John 9 had no way of knowing when he got up that morning that he was about to regain his eyesight. The same goes for the lame man in Acts 3. As a general rule, those who received miracles in the Bible were given no advance notice. The forces of heaven are released "suddenly" – as He wills!

The prophet Elijah possessed the Gift of Working of Miracles in abundance. Remember when he prayed and it did not rain for the space of three years! It brought about a great drought in the land (1 Kings 17-19). Then later, He prayed again and it rained! It was during this period of drought that he came to a widow and asked her to give him something to eat. She told Elijah that she and her son had only enough oil and enough meal to make some bread for themselves. They were going to eat it and then wait to die. Let's examine this story more closely...

1 Kings chapter 17 reports that the Lord was withholding rain from Israel (verse 1). In verse 8, the Lord commanded Elijah to go to Zarephath, a town outside of Israel, where a widow would provide food for him. He obeyed, finding a woman gathering sticks. He said to her, *"Bring me a little water in a vessel, that I may drink,"* and, *"Bring me a morsel of bread in your hand"* (verses 11–12). The widow, however, was in great need herself. She responded, *"As the Lord your God lives, I have nothing baked, only a handful of flour*

in a jar and a little oil in a jug. And now I am gathering a couple of sticks that I may go in and prepare it for myself and my son, that we may eat it and die" (verse 13). She expected the meal she was about to prepare to be the last for her and her family. She had no other option than to die of starvation.

Elijah's answer was surely a test of her faith. He told her that she was to make some food for him. Anyway, using the last of her ingredients she obeyed, and he added a promise: "For thus says the Lord, the God of Israel, 'The jar of flour shall not be spent, and the jug of oil shall not be empty, until the day that the Lord sends rain upon the earth'" (1 Kings 17:14). The widow's faith was marked by her obedience. God was faithful to His promise: "She and he and her household ate for many days. The jar of flour was not spent, neither did the jug of oil become empty, according to the word of the Lord that he spoke by Elijah" (verses 15–16). The widow's food supply was supernaturally extended, exactly the way God had promised. This is very similar to Jesus feeding the five thousand, as recorded in all four Gospels.

Aside from the resurrection, the story of Jesus feeding the 5,000 is the only miracle recorded in all four Gospels. Obviously, the writers must have considered this a significant miracle.

When Christ fed the masses that day, He began with only "five barley loaves and two fish," borrowed from a boy's lunch (John 6:9). To feed 5,000 people with five loaves and two fish is indeed miraculous, but the Greek term used in Matthew 14:21 specifies males, and Matthew further emphasises the point by adding, "Besides women and children." Many Bible scholars believe the actual number fed that day could have been between 15,000—20,000 people.

Jesus' disciples had wanted to send the people away because evening was approaching, and they were in a remote place. They knew that the people needed to reach surrounding villages soon in order to buy food, find lodging, etc., or they would likely go hungry. However, Jesus had a better idea: "You give them something to eat" (Matthew 14:16). At this point, the disciples should have recalled the many miracles they had seen Jesus do. Perhaps some of them did, but

Andrew asked, *"What can five loaves and two fish do for so many?"* Philip exclaimed, *"It would take more than half a year's wages to buy enough bread for each to eat!"*

Jesus called for the bread and fish to be brought to Him. He then gave thanks for the meal, broke the bread, and handed it to His disciples for distribution to the crowd. Astonishingly, the entire multitude was fed with that small amount of food. The Lord provided *"as much as they wanted"* (John 6:11), and *"they all ate and were satisfied"* (Matthew 14:20). Jesus didn't just meet their need, He lavished them with so much food that there were *"twelve baskets full of broken pieces and of the fish"* left over. It is worth noting that this miracle came about as the disciples dispersed the food. Often, your miracle comes from what you have in your own hand!

We are all familiar with the other miracles Jesus performed in... *Turning the water into wine; walking on the water; stilling the storm; raising the dead; etc.* But what about other men who were filled with the Spirit? When Paul was writing to the Corinthians, defending the title of apostle, he said to them in 2 Corinthians 12:12, *"Truly the signs of an apostle were wrought among you in all patience, **in signs and wonders and mighty deeds.**"* So Paul is pointing to the miracles that were done through his ministry while he was there in Corinth. He used those as a sign to validate the fact that he was an apostle. Hence, it would seem that one of the requirements of apostleship in the early church was to have the Gift of Working of Miracles in operation.

However, the Gift of the Working of Miracles, in the early church, was not limited to the apostles. When Paul (Saul) was on the way to Damascus to imprison those who were calling upon the name of Jesus, he had an encounter whereby the Lord spoke to him and called him into full-time service. As a result of this encounter with Jesus, he was blinded and had to be led into Damascus. There we find a certain disciple of Jesus (in Damascus) whose name was Ananias. He was not an apostle, just a disciple. In Acts 9, the Lord spoke to him and told him to go to the street called Straight, to inquire at the house of Simon for this man Saul. So Ananias came and said, *"Saul,* the Lord has sent me to you that you might receive your sight and be filled with the Holy Spirit." So, he laid hands on Paul, and Paul received his sight and was **filled** with the Holy Spirit. God can use anyone to perform miracles! There is no exclusivity or monopoly in this area of ministry. All that is required is submission and obedience – as with all the *gifts*! The question remains, "Do you believe God can use you?"

Not only can the Gifts of the Holy Spirit operate through any believer (often functioning together), they can also manifest through two people at the same time. Let me explain...

I was once visiting a church in north London with a close friend. Being a seasoned minister, my friend took the service and I was there to support him. We often did this and were led by the Spirit as to how to minister to people's needs at the end. This time, I got a Word of Knowledge about someone in attendance that had a leg shorter than the other. The moment I revealed it, my friend said "it is a woman." I immediately followed by stating that it was a woman with red hair. Strangely, each time we spoke, no one responded. My friend continued... "It is a woman who is an athlete." I continued, "And it's due to your training that your one leg has become shorter than the other."

A red haired woman in her early twenties came running forward! Before proceeding to pray for her, we sat her on a chair to make sure the one leg was shorter than the other. It's quite easy to determine when you sit in a chair with your back straight and your legs parallel to the ground. Sure enough, the one leg was about an inch and a half shorter than the other. Had the young woman continued, her athletics career would have ended with serious back problems. Well... We both laid our hands on her, and immediately, her leg grew out in front of everyone's eyes! The place erupted! And God was glorified.

The Bible is full of miraculous displays of God's power, but what is happening in the church today? No one should question the power of God to work extraordinary miracles. After all, He's God! He can invade our lives at any time He chooses - to do things that we cannot comprehend. It's not God's power that's the issue, and it's not our belief in miracles (past or present).

Furthermore, the problem is not whether we believe in miracles or, what kind of miracles we may believe in. The problem lies with our limited understanding of how God works - especially with regards the Gifts of the Holy Spirit, and the one *gift* that is probably the most challenging for the modern church is the Gift of the Working of Miracles! In that respect, the biggest test of our faith would be to have someone raised from the dead by the power of God. Yet, that should not be the issue! God is a miracle-working God, who has no limitations, and with whom nothing is impossible! Here are eight accounts, documented in the Bible of people being raised from the dead:

1. **The Widow of Zarephath's Son.** The prophet Elijah had been lodging at the house of a widow in Zarephath, a pagan city. Unexpectedly, the woman's son grew sick and died. She accused Elijah of bringing God's wrath on her for her sin. Carrying the boy to the upper room where he was staying, Elijah stretched himself out on the dead body three times. He then cried out to God for the boy's life to return. God heard Elijah's prayers, and the child's life did come back, and Elijah carried him downstairs. The woman declared the prophet a man of God and his words to be the truth (1 Kings 17:17-24).

2. **The Shunammite Woman's Son.** Elisha, the prophet after Elijah, stayed in the upper room of a couple in Shunem. He prayed for the woman to bear a son, and God answered. Several years later, the boy complained of a pain in his head and then died. The woman raced to Mount Carmel to Elisha, who sent his servant ahead, but the boy did not respond. Elisha went in, cried out to the Lord, and laid himself on the dead body. The boy sneezed seven times and opened his eyes. When Elisha presented the boy back to his mother, she fell and bowed to the ground (2 Kings 4:18-37).

3. **The Israelite Man.** After Elisha the prophet died, he was buried in a tomb. Moabite raiders attacked Israel every

spring, one time interrupting a funeral. Fearing for their own lives, the burial party quickly threw the body into the first convenient place, Elisha's tomb. As soon as the body touched Elisha's bones, the dead man came to life and stood up. This miracle was probably a foretelling of how Christ's death and resurrection turned the grave into the passageway to new life (2 Kings 13:20-21).

4. **The Widow of Nain's Son.** At the town gate of the village of Nain, Jesus and his disciples encountered a funeral procession. The only son of a widow was to be buried. Jesus' heart went out to her. He touched the stretcher that held the body, and the bearers stopped. When Jesus told the young man to get up, the son sat up and began talking. Jesus gave him back to his mother. All the people were astounded. Praising God, they said, *"A great prophet has appeared among us. God has come to help his people"* (Luke 7:11-17).

5. **Jairus' Daughter.** When Jesus was in Capernaum, Jairus, a leader in the synagogue, begged him to heal his 12 year-old daughter because she was dying. On the way, a messenger said not to bother because the girl had died. Jesus arrived at the house to find mourners wailing outside. When he said she was not dead but sleeping, they laughed at him. Jesus went in, took her by the hand and said, "My child, get up." Her spirit returned, and she lived. Jesus ordered her parents to give her something to eat but not to tell anyone what had happened (Luke 8:49-56).

6. **Lazarus.** Three of Jesus' closest friends were Martha, Mary, and their brother Lazarus of Bethany. Oddly, when Jesus was told Lazarus was sick, Jesus stayed two more days where he was. When he left, Jesus knew Lazarus had died. Martha met them outside the village, where Jesus told her, "Your brother will rise again. I am the resurrection and the life."

They approached the tomb, where Jesus wept. Although Lazarus had been dead four days, Jesus ordered the stone rolled away. Raising his eyes to heaven, he prayed aloud to his

Father. Then, He commanded Lazarus to come out. The man who had been dead for 4 days walked out, wrapped in burial cloths (John 11:1-44).

7. **Tabitha (or Dorkas).** Everyone in the city of Joppa loved Tabitha. She was always doing good, helping the poor, and making garments for others. One day Tabitha (named Dorcas in Greek) grew sick and died. Women washed her body then placed it in an upstairs room. They sent for the apostle Peter, who was in nearby Lydda. Clearing everyone from the room, Peter fell to his knees and prayed. He said to her, *"Tabitha, get up."* She sat up and Peter gave her to her friends alive. News spread like wildfire. Many people believed in Jesus because of it (Acts 9:36-42).

8. **Eutychus.** It was a packed third story room in Troas. The hour was late, many oil lamps made the quarters warm, and the apostle Paul spoke on and on. Sitting on a windowsill, the young man Eutychus dozed off, falling out of the window to his death. Paul rushed outside and threw himself on the lifeless body. Immediately, Eutychus came back to life. Paul went back upstairs, broke bread and ate. The people, relieved, took Eutychus home alive (Acts 20:7-12).

It's interesting to note that four of the eight people raised from the dead were children, and two of them were widows sons'. God responds to the heart-cry of a grieving mother's heart! We should never rule out a **miracle**, even when we are confronted by death. For if we do, we are not accommodating the truth that God is the Almighty, and with Him all things are possible. *"For with God nothing will be impossible"* (Luke 1:37). This must include raising the dead! I find it difficult to accept that any Christian would choose not to believe in miracles.

In New Testament times, there were many eyewitnesses who saw miracles, signs and wonders, so they could not deny that miracles were performed. Yet, when Jesus did an astounding miracle in Matthew 12:22-24, the religious authorities would not accept that a miracle had been done by Jesus. Instead, they attributed it to the power of Beelzebub rather than God. Yet, they still acknowledged the miracle! Can you see something? Miracles were irrefutable and undeniable.

The word "miracles" means *"power, or inherent ability,"* and *"is used of works of a supernatural origin and character, such as could not be produced by natural agents and means"* (W.E. Vine, Expository Dictionary). Therefore, the birth of a baby or the unfolding of a flower, both natural events, cannot be classified as miracles. The birth of Jesus, on the other hand, was a miracle. It is not natural for a woman who has not known a man (that is, had physical contact with one) to have a child. The start of everything we believe today was established in an environment of miracles.

God can and does provide miracles for people in need, even for unbelievers, because He loves them. It was the same in Bible times; *"the whole multitude sought to touch (Jesus), for power went out from Him, and healed them all"* Luke 6:19. Yet, the ones who saw miracles every day were those who were with Him all the time. Rather than living our own lives, ignoring Jesus and then coming to Him when we need a miracle, we should enter into a close personal relationship with Him, following Him every day. Then we will see the most astounding miracle of all - as we are changed daily to become more like Him. Becoming more like Jesus is a transformation that is probably the greatest miracle of all!

"A miracle is a supernatural intervention in the ordinary course of nature, a temporary suspension of the accustomed order through the Spirit of God."

Kenneth Hagin

8

The Gift of Prophecy

The Gift of Prophecy is an extraordinary and unique spiritual gift, given to the Church to edify, encourage and comfort everyone present. The apostle Paul says in 1 Corinthians 14:1 to *"Pursue love, and earnestly desire the spiritual gifts, especially that you may prophesy."* This *gift* is a blessing to the Church and should not be quenched or despised (1 Thessalonians 5:20). Remember, no matter what vessel God's Spirit may use to manifest the Gift of Prophecy, it will operate differently from the *gift* given to the Old Testament prophets. The "prophets of old" spoke an authoritative word direct from God and the prophecy could not be altered or misrepresented in any way. In fact, if this happened they risked being called false prophets and put to death (Deuteronomy 13:13).

The words of the Old Testament prophets were not necessarily meant to edify, encourage or comfort the hearer. Instead, they were words God Himself was communicating without ambiguity. These prophecies usually comprised of a specific and enduring message from the Almighty - to a certain individual or particular group of people. Such revelations may have been conditional, or they were direct statements from God. They may even contain detailed descriptions or information concerning future events.

This makes the Old Testament prophets very different from anyone presently being used to manifest the Gift of Prophecy in church. Too many Christians are ignorant of this fact. They think there is a direct correlation between the Old Testament prophets and the *gift* mentioned in 1 Corinthians 12. Yes, there may be some similarities with the office of the *prophet*, as listed in Ephesians 4:11 (*the five-fold ministry gifts*), because the New Testament prophet is like the rudder of a ship, constantly at work navigating the vessel. Always adjusting the course in order to avoid disaster. However, we need to keep the old separate from the new! Primarily, because the Holy Spirit now dwells in all believers. Hence, every believer has the ability to hear the voice of God without having to wait for the prophet to speak.

We should also realise that the words of the prophets were recorded as Holy Scripture, as they proclaimed, *"Thus says The Lord"* whereas the messages from those operating in the Gift of Prophecy need to be *tested* (1 Corinthians 14:29-33; 1 Thessalonians 5:20-21; 1 John 4:1-3). In the New Testament, it is 'the saints', not the prophets, who have taken over the role of scriptural proclamation and revelation. So, let's stop applying Old Testament principles to modern day prophecy! This only opens people up to superstitious practices and encourages new-age mysticism to circulate in the church. Over the years, I have seen some very strange attempts to manifest the Gift of Prophecy. If it wasn't so dangerous, it would be laughable!

It seems that everyone wants to be a modern-day prophet! A spiritual guru who can foretell the future and see into the soul of man. However, this is not spiritual, it's carnal. Just because people love to read their horoscopes (to see what should be happening in their lives), does not mean we should mimic it with something that appears spiritual and bring it into the church.

I remember going to a church in England where the leaders put out a mike, on a stand in front of the podium, and encouraged people to come out and prophesy. You would not believe some of the things that were verbalised! The favourite style or pattern of such 'prophecies' is where people reveal what they "see!" Things like, "I see moonbeams bouncing off a peaceful stream and casting a shadow onto an unmanned boat." Or, "I see someone walking in a field of unharvested wheat and light is radiating from all around him." These two sentences, I have just made up, but they do appear quite spiritual... Don't they? Here are some real 'prophecies' I have heard in churches. "I see a billiard table with only the black ball left. Suddenly it catapults itself into the far right-hand corner." Lastly, "I see a doughnut that is being filled with delicious jam and cream."

None of the above have the slightest ability to *edify, encourage* or *comfort*. They are ambiguous, confusing and perplexing. God does not speak to us in coded images. He speaks to us by His Spirit – Spirit to spirit! And when God speaks it will always make perfect sense, even if we don't fully understand it at that moment in time. It's hard enough trying to navigate through the storms of life without the Lord giving us encrypted messages. In Acts 9:10-12, we see clearly how God speaks. *In Damascus, there was a disciple named Ananias. The Lord called to him in a vision, "Ananias!" "Yes, Lord," he answered. The Lord told him, "Go to the house of Judas on Straight Street and ask for a man from Tarsus named Saul, for he is praying. In a vision he has seen a man named Ananias come and place his hands on him to restore his sight."*

Can you imagine what would have happened if God spoke to Ananias by using confusing dialog and blurred information? Saul would never have become Paul, and the New Testament would never have contained all the Epistles this great man had written.

The Greek word for prophecy is 'propheteia' (προφητεία), which is the ability to receive a divinely inspired message that can be delivered to others in the church. The noun is in the feminine, which implies vulnerability and sensitivity, and confirms how the prophecy ought to be delivered. It is the gift of communicating and conveying revealed truth. As stated, these messages should always conform to the essential prerequisite of exhortation, encouragement, and comfort. That way, the Body of Christ may be **built up** (1 Corinthians 14:3-4, 24-25). Again, they do not, and will never, constitute the authoritative Word of God. They are simply human interpretations of *revelations* that were received from God's Spirit. Therefore, they may be flawed. Remember, a prophecy is spoken in human words and expressed through a human mind, which is why it needs to be tested against the Scriptures (1 Thessalonians 5:20-21).

In the Old Testament the Holy Spirit came upon three anointed vessels; the king, the high priest, and the prophet. Today, we all have the Holy Spirit inside of us. Therefore, any words spoken over us should resonate within us. If you don't witness with what has been spoken over you - just shelve it! Moreover, if you feel it is totally false, let the person prophesying know! Don't ever say "Amen" to what you disagree with! We are to be very cautious of those who claim to have a "new" message from God. It is one thing to say, "I had an interesting dream last night." However, it is quite another matter to say, "God gave me a dream last night, and you must accept it." No utterance of man should ever be considered equal to, or above, the written Word. We must hold onto the infallible Word that God has already given and commit ourselves to Scripture alone. That is our only safeguard.

We cannot afford to despise the Gift of Prophecy, nor can we allow its capacity for misuse and misunderstanding to prevent us from embracing it.

Rather we must diligently seek to curb its abuses by applying the guidelines of Scripture, and *"test all things"* (1 Thessalonians 5:20-21). That way, the constructive value of prophecy may be experienced by our churches. Through this unique *spiritual gift* the church is empowered to grow, mature and move forward according to the will of God. *"Make love your aim, and earnestly desire the spiritual gifts, especially that you may prophesy ... so that the church may be edified"* (1 Corinthians 14:1, 5).

The Holy Spirit gives the Gift of Prophecy to believers to make God's heart known and to *edify* the church. This *gift* is for the benefit of both believers and unbelievers, as it is a sign that God is actually present among His people (1 Corinthians 14:22-25). Those who genuinely operate in this gift are sensitive to both the prompting of the Holy Spirit and the needs of the church body. They are humble and constantly study the Word in order to "test" their own revelations before speaking them publicly. When they do speak, they should allow, and even expect others to weigh what is said against the Scriptures and interpret the message accordingly. In this way, the church may be continually built up in unity (1 Corinthians 14:4, 26).

Edification, encouragement and *assurance* are the primary reasons the spiritual Gift of Prophecy will manifest in the church. In 1 Corinthians 14:3, the apostle Paul contrasts *tongues* (a God-ward speaking), with *prophecy* (a man-ward message): *"He who prophesies speaks to men for their edification* (οἰκοδομή) *and encouragement* (παράκλησιν) *and comfort* (παραμυθίαν)*."* Encouragement (παράκλησιν) has a wide range of meaning. Its root carries the idea *"to call alongside to help"*, as in Another Helper (John 14:16). Additionally, the word can denote *"exhortation."* It also extends to the idea of *"comfort or consolation"* (Romans 15:4; Colossians 4:8; and 2 Corinthians 1:3).

Notice, the fundamentally significant way that the Holy Spirit is fulfilling the ministry of 'παράκλησιν' is through the *exhortation, edification* and *comforting assurance* of the Gift of Prophecy.

Let us now consider an area of prophecy that we do not hear much about: the impact of prophecy on those who are not walking right with God – the unbeliever:

> *"But if all prophesy, and an **unbeliever** or an uninformed person comes in, he is convinced by all, he is **convicted** by all. And thus the secrets of his heart are revealed; and so, falling down on his face, he will worship God and report that God is truly among you"* (1 Corinthians 14:24-25).

Let us examine the four key words in the passage. (1) The word **convinced** comes from the Greek word meaning *"to admonish, convince, rebuke, or reprove."* (2) The Greek word **convicted** means *"to scrutinize, investigate, determine, discern, search."* (3) The word **secrets** means *"concealed, private, or hidden."* (4) The word **revealed** is from a word meaning *"manifest, apparent, visible, conspicuous."* Putting all these words together we can assume that this passage is telling us that the Gift of Prophecy can communicate directly to the hearts of the unbeliever and unenlightened in such a way that they will be admonished and convicted. The message flowing out of the prophecy will impact on their hearts and minds, and cause them to turn to God – worshipping Him! The Gift of Prophecy in operation is a sign that Jesus dwells in the midst of His people: *"Worship God! For the testimony of Jesus is the spirit of prophecy"* (Revelation 19:10).

When we gather together (have ἐκκλησία), we should consider "those who are without." We ought to be gathering together to seek out opportunities, and work in cooperation with the Holy Spirit, to reach and transform the 'unenlightened'.

That way, we may influence the people around us in a positive way! Whenever we are "connected" and "in touch" with the Holy Spirit, there will always flow a positive message from the heart of God to those listening. If the Holy Spirit is allowed to have His way in our churches, He will speak edification and encouragement to the listener and bring glory to Jesus Christ!

Let's now examine the Gift of Prophecy in the Book of Acts (Acts 2:16). The setting... it's the day of Pentecost, 50 days after the resurrection of Jesus Christ. There are 120 men and women waiting in the upper room to be *"clothed with power from on high"* (Luke 24:49). According to Acts 2:2, the Holy Spirit comes in like the sound of a rushing wind. In verse 4 Luke says, *"they were all **filled** with the Holy Spirit and began to speak in other tongues."* Verse 11 is more exact about what they were speaking. Some of the foreigners who heard them said, *"We hear them telling in our own tongues the mighty works of God."* Note, the topic of their words was very specific – to testify concerning the mighty works of God. If we are to fully comprehend the true nature of the Gift of Prophecy, this is important to us.

In verse 16, Peter explains what is actually taking place. He says, this is what was spoken by the prophet Joel. In fact, that was the beginning of the fulfilment of Joel 2:28.

Peter proceeds to quote Joel (verses 17–18), *"And in the last days it shall be, God declares, that I will pour out my Spirit upon all flesh, and your sons and your daughters shall prophesy, and your young men shall see visions, and your old men shall dream dreams; yea, and on my menservants and my maidservants in those days I will pour out my Spirit; and they shall **prophesy.**"*

Joel had declared that in the last days there would be a great outpouring of the Spirit "on all flesh," and the mark of that outpouring would be widespread prophesying.

Peter's sermon ends in Acts 2:39, declaring… *"The promise (of the Spirit in verse 38) is to you and to your children and to all that are far off, every one whom the Lord our God calls to Him."* Notice, the promised includes men and women, old and young, low class and upper class. Isn't that encouraging? All of God's children shall prophesy in the last days (the days we are living in now), and this will become a worldwide phenomenon. Why? Because God is pouring out His Holy Spirit on "all flesh," and He desires to communicate important messages throughout this entire process. Hence, one manifestation of the Spirit of God in the last days will be a surprising widespread Gift of Prophecy (verses 17-18).

In the early church, once the outpouring had started, the Gift of Prophecy spread to the average person (as prophesied in Joel). Acts 21:9 tells of Philip's four daughters, *"And the same man had four daughters, **virgins**, which did all **prophesy.**"* Note, they were not prophets, yet they prophesied. They had a distinct ministry of *edifying* and *encouraging* the church. However, they did not foretell the future. Furthermore, the four daughters were virgins. In this regard, the word "virgin" not only means that they were as yet unmarried, it reveals the fact that these women had devoted themselves fully (if not by irrevocable vows) to a form of holy service to God. They had found a steadfast purpose, and that was, to edify and encourage the church. In the organisation and administration of women's work (in the early church), they apparently represented a distinct and very respected class of ministry. Oh how we need such dedicated young people today! Young men and women who feel called to *edify* and *encourage* the church and are prepared to dedicate their lives to that service. The fact that these women were all yet unmarried (still virgins) reflects the level of devotion and duty they had to God and His kingdom.

At this juncture in our study, what can we confidently ascertain concerning the Gift of Prophecy in the modern church? Is it still valid, effective and useful to us? 1 Corinthians 13:8-12 and Acts 2:17-18 jointly indicate that it definitely is. The Gift of Prophecy is a Spirit-prompted, Spirit-sustained utterance that is rooted and established in true revelation (1 Corinthians 14:30). Yet, although embedded in such an infallible source (the Bible), it is still mortal and imperfect. Why? Because it is "uttered" through flawed vessels! Still, it is very useful to the church. The spiritual *gift* of prophecy is primarily one of proclamation ("forth-telling") and not prediction ("fore-telling"). It ought to be desired and appreciated by all believers. Let's now determine what prophecy *is not*!

The Gift of Prophecy is not...

- *Foretelling the future.* There is never any foretelling or predicting the future. This practice is dangerous because it can lead to a form of divination that is steeped in falsity and superstition. Yet, many church goers have a strange fascination for such matters.

- *A ministry of guidance.* Guidance or direction is not one of the operations of the *gift* of prophecy. As mentioned earlier, this is reserved for the office of the Prophet (as understood in the Old Testament and in Ephesians 4:11).

- *A ministry of preaching.* Preaching means to proclaim and pronounce the Good News, that is the Gospel of Jesus Christ, and it proceeds out of the natural mind and not the spirit. Prophecy however, is the mind of the Holy Spirit speaking to us in a supernatural utterance.

- *A ministry of rebuke.* There is no element of rebuke in prophecy, as it is centred around encouragement and edification. This should be discouraged at all times.

- *A ministry of criticism.* Prophecy is not one person's opinion or disapproval of or against another. It is a divine operation under the anointing of God's Spirit designed to convict believers of sin or shortcomings (getting them in line with the Word of God), for the purpose of building them up – not tearing them down!

- *Without guidelines.* First Corinthians 14:29 tells how the gift of prophecy is regulated: *"Let the prophets speak two or three, and let the other judge."* There should be, at the most, three messages of prophecy in one church meeting. Even if you should feel a notion to prophesy, you should discard it if God has already spoken three times. Verse 33 tells us how this precious gift can be safeguarded and protected, *"for God is not the author of confusion, but of peace."*

- *Independent of the Spirit of God.* It is not a *gift* you can function in without the leading of the Spirit of God. It is operated and manifested only "as He wills."

1 Thessalonians 5:20 tells us plainly not to despise prophecy. Some pastors and ministers do not want this *gift* to function in their churches because they cannot personally control it. We must accept, when dealing with the supernatural, that there will always be a certain element of vulnerability involved. When the Gifts of the Spirit are not being executed properly, they can be a danger. The *gifts* of the Spirit have a proper place and a proper time to function, and are entirely under His divine authority and control.

Here are some practical suggestions when operating in the gifts:

1. *Recognise God's sovereignty.* God gives *gifts* freely to whoever He wills (1 Corinthians 12:11; Hebrews 2:4).

2. *Recognise boundaries and callings.* Not all who prophesy suddenly become prophets (1 Corinthians 12:29).

3. *Recognise that love is the driving force.* Make love your aim in all things, realising that love is the greatest miracle and the surest sign of God's blessing (1 Corinthians 14:1, 12, 26, 37; 2:14).

4. *Recognise that humility opens the door to ministry.* Have humble expectations that the prophecy will not be taken as a word of Scripture but as a Spirit-prompted human word to be weighed by Scripture.

5. *Recognise that the gifts are not for self-promotion or exhibition.* All the *gifts* are meant to bring glory to God the Father and Jesus Christ alone. Hence, no one should attempt to divert the glory to himself!

6. *Recognise the need for spiritual maturity.* For a prophecy to be accepted as valid it should find an echo in the hearts of spiritually mature people. They should "witness" with it, and the prophecy ought to be confirmed through biblical and mature discernment (1 Thessalonians 5:19; Colossians 1:9; 3:15; Ephesians 5:15-17; Romans 12:1-2; Philippians 1:9-10). Amen

Prophecy by Christopher Lodewyk
Given to Cornerstone The Church

I am pleased with you says The Lord, and I announce My pleasure, because I have a unique task for you.

Do not treat it lightly, but continue to bring pleasure and joy to My own heart, says The Lord.

Just as my Father said, this is my Son, so I say these are My people.

I have called you to be My people that bring pleasure and I announce it for the purpose that you may continue to do the unique, continue to do (that) which others at times seek to achieve.

I have called you for a special purpose, I have called you to, to implore your efforts, your hearts and your minds to do that which others fear to do, because I have found in you the pleasure that I have in My Church.

Do not take it lightly says the Lord, but continue to please Me, because it is the highest form of worship.

I need you at this time says the Lord, to perform that which others seek and struggle to perform or achieve, and highlight and prioritise. For that reason, seek My face, seek My guidance, continue to be led by Me so that I may achieve all and everything that I seek to achieve through you. So that you may continue to bring joy and pleasure to My heart says The Lord.

Amen

9

The Gift of Discerning Of Spirits

ἄλλῳ διακρίσεις πνευμάτων

It's interesting to note that the ancient Greek word translated "discerning" (διακρίσεις) represents an act of judgement. It literally means *"to pass sentence on."* It is a discernment that brings about a verdict – *causes one to conclude*. It distinguishes that which is real or true from that which is false or untrue. It exposes the "look-alikes" (the things that appear to be the same). It sheds light on deceitful, dishonest, sinful and insincere opinions and practices. It brings judgement on all the workings of evil. Furthermore because this *gift* is spiritual (concerning spirits) it causes one to 'see clearly' in order to pass sentence on everything that is anti-Christ. Notice, that the main emphasis of this *gift* is to expose the works of the devil; *"The one who practices sin [separating himself from God, and offending Him by acts of disobedience, indifference, or rebellion] is of the devil [and takes his inner character and moral values from him, not God]; for the devil has sinned and violated God's law from the beginning. The Son of God appeared for this purpose, to destroy the works of the devil"* (1 John 3:8).

The Discerning of Spirits is mentioned immediately after the Gift of Prophecy, which provides a direct clue as to one of its functions. It's the spiritual ability to determine between genuine revelation from God and that which is false – a lying or deceiving spirit. When someone voices a prophecy, it's necessary to quickly determine whether or not that prophecy is in fact an utterance from God. So, the Lord supernaturally gifts some individuals with the discernment to determine whether the message was from Him, or from that person's own imagination, or a false message from satan. The Bible warns us of satan's deceptions, and no wonder! For satan transforms himself into an angel of light (2 Corinthians 11:14). We really need this *gift* to operate in its fullness in the church! We ought to be able to "pass judgement" (διακρίσεις) on all those evil spirits that are behind practices intended to bring confusion and division.

Observe, the *gift* of the Discerning of Spirits allows you to 'see' what is hidden beyond the natural appearance of things in order to expose the spirit behind them. The 'seeing' is not necessarily a vision of what is actually manifest in the spirit realm (although it can be), it is more likely to be a supernatural and spontaneous 'knowing' inspired by the Holy Spirit. I have heard of great men of God who have been permitted to 'see' into the realm of the spirit in order to deal with certain situations, but very few can be trusted with such a profound experience. So, we should not be seeking visions! This provides the devil with opportunities to deceive and lead us astray.

We must also be aware that there are spirits operating, and these spirits control or function through people. That is why the *gift* of the Discerning of Spirits is necessary to build and edify the church today. Without it, we could not 'see' the works of the devil and would not know how to deal with his evil schemes.

What I have found most common in church circles today is the *religious spirit*. It is the most prominent and most visible "look-alike" spirit. It masquerades as an angel of light! Like the devil himself, it is centred in pride. The sheer arrogance of this spirit never ceases to amaze me! It is a spirit of deception and the people it is operating through are therefore deceived. The other prominent spirit in church today is the judgemental spirit. Notice, how this spirit is trying to mimic "διακρίσεις" - the gift to *bring judgement upon and pass sentence on*. It has already concluded that matters are not in line with its evil agenda and has brought about its own unjust verdict. Remember, the Spirit of God never condemns, *for there is no condemnation for those in Christ Jesus* (Romans 8:1).

When this *gift* expresses itself, the Holy Spirit provides super-natural discernment, insight, and knowledge concerning various kinds of spirits. The believer who is operating in this *gift* is used to fully expose what is going on and who is being employed behind the natural order of things. He becomes a "seer" of sorts and reveals the true identity of anyone or anything God wants the church to be aware of.

The *gift* of the Discerning of Spirits is one that is really needed in the dangerous and perilous times that we live in. Remember, the word "spirits" is plural and is with a small "s." This means that it is not referring to the Holy Spirit but other types of spirits at work in the earth. Therefore, this *gift* is meant to reveal one of the following three categories of spirits:

1. Demonic spirits

2. God's angels

3. Human spirits

Here is how this *gift* transacts with each of these different kinds of spirits.

-   **Demonic Spirits** - with demonic spirits still being allowed to exercise authority (in the air and on the earth) and also to intermingle with us to some degree, we really need this *gift* in full operation today. Ephesians 6:2 tells us that, *"We do not wrestle against flesh and blood, but against principalities, against powers, against the rulers of the darkness of this age, against spiritual hosts of wickedness in the heavenly places"*. As you know, many times demons can literally enter into a person's body (take possession) if they have the legal right to do so.

In the physical realm, all spirits need a 'body' through which to operate. Unlike the Spirit of God, who desires to be noticed and understood, evil spirits will try to hide and not show themselves. They are cunning and will use all forms of deception to stay in control. That is why Jesus delivered people from the oppression of the devil (Acts 10:38). The *gift* of the Discerning of Spirits was evident in Jesus' ministry, and evil spirits recognised and submitted to His authority. They even called Him Lord!

"Night and day, he was in the mountains and in the tombs, crying out and cutting himself with stones. When he saw Jesus from afar, he ran and worshiped Him. And he cried out with a loud voice and said, "What have I to do with You, Jesus, Son of the Most High God? I implore You by God that You do not torment me." For He said to him, "Come out of the man, unclean spirit!" Then He asked him, "What is your name?" He answered, saying, "My name is Legion; for we are many." Also he begged Him earnestly that He would not send them out of the country. - Mark 5:5-10.

Jesus was able to deliver this man of two thousand evil spirits!

Now a large herd of swine was feeding there near the mountains. So all the demons begged Him, saying, "Send us to the swine, that we may enter them." And at once Jesus gave them permission. Then the unclean spirits went out and entered the swine (there were about two thousand); and the herd ran violently down the steep place into the sea, and drowned in the sea. (verses 11-13).

If Jesus wasn't aware of the unclean spirits, and if they were not aware of Him, the outcome would have been totally different. That is why we need the same gift and the same Spirit at work in and through us!

The Great Commission includes an instruction to cast out demons. *"And these signs will follow those who believe: In My name they will cast out demons; they will speak with* new tongues; they will take up serpents; and if they drink anything deadly, it will by no means hurt them; they will lay hands on the sick, and they will recover" (Mark 16:17-18). The question remains... Can a believer cast out something he is unaware of? Hence, the absolute necessity to have the *gift* of the Discerning of Spirits in large supply.

- **God's Angels** - The Bible tells us that God's angels are also spirit beings. *"Who makes His angels spirit, and His ministers a flame of fire"* (Hebrews 1:7). They are all ministering spirits, sent forth to minister for those who will inherit salvation (Hebrews 1:14). Throughout history God's angels have appeared to people. The Bible is full of such supernatural interventions. There are roughly 300 references to angels in scripture. One hundred and four of them are manifestations and visitations to men and women.

Yet not one of those people mentioned was praying to see an angel when it occurred. So be careful, "If you pray to see an angel, satan will gladly accommodate you." He may even send an unclean spirit disguised as an angel of light to deceive you and lead you into catastrophe. One of the leading false religions in the world came about as a result of an angel "teaching" a man from Vermont a foolish revelation that is not in God's Word. Of course, that was a counterfeit fallen-angel, but the man was so ignorant of the things of God that he did not know the difference. As a result, he proceeded to build a world-wide religion based on the angel having deceived him.

When dealing with the supernatural, particularly the ministry of angels, some believers have a tendency to go overboard. The apostle Paul said they end up deceiving themselves. They get entangled in all kinds of problems because they did not bother to study the instructions provided in God's Word. There is no mention in God's Word of any *female* angels. They are always referred to as *male* - in the masculine tense. There appears to be two female angels in the Book of Zechariah (chapter 5:9-11), however, these are not angels at all. Rather, they are demonic instruments in God's hands sent to bring judgment on the nation of Israel by bringing them into captivity as a result of their sins. Most commentators and translators agree that these two "women" are evil spirits and that the *"wind in their wings"* denotes the swiftness with which they would bring judgment to Israel. So, be careful when someone tells you a female angel has appeared to them. There are numerous references to the *feminine* in God's Word, but this is not one of them.

Angels cannot replace the teaching ministry of the Holy Spirit. Angels cannot live inside of you, and human beings do not become angels when they die. Angels can, however, cause circumstances to turn in your favour. They can provide supernatural manifestations of love, comfort and freedom. They can perform amazing feats of strength and operate in the supernatural. However, they cannot teach and preach the Gospel, and it is rare indeed that they bring guidance to a believer. That is because guidance is what the Spirit of God does. *For when He, the Spirit of truth comes, He will guide you into all truth* (John 16:13).

Once again, no one but the Holy Spirit is able to truly control supernatural manifestations. Therefore, do not pray for them, for the devil may accommodate you. If an angel were to suddenly appear, the first thing you will need to do is properly discern the spirits. John tells us exactly how to do this.

"Beloved, do not believe every spirit, but test the spirits, whether they are of God; because many false prophets have gone out into the world. By this you know the Spirit of God: Every spirit that confesses that Jesus Christ has come in the flesh is of God, and every spirit that does not confess that Jesus Christ has come in the flesh is not of God. And this is the spirit of the Antichrist, which you have heard was coming, and is now already in the world. You are of God, little children, and have overcome them, because He who is in you is greater than he who is in the world" (1 John 4:1-4).

Judge all supernatural manifestations according to the written Word of God. Be fully dependent on the Holy Spirit, and keep your eyes on Jesus. Not on angels!

- **Human Spirits** - in addition to angels and demonic spirits, the third kind of spirit is the human spirit. This is where *humanism* and many *new-age* practices originate. The one pretends not to be spiritual, and the other, pretends to be spiritual. Yet, they are both merely "look-alikes." That is why we need to discern them correctly. The English Dictionary defines humanism as *'a rationalist outlook of thought attaching prime importance to human rather than divine or supernatural matters'*. This belief system promotes the kingdom of "self." We know the devil rules in that jurisdiction because 'self' and 'pride' are one and the same. So, don't let anyone fool you by saying humanism, or philosophy, are not spiritual.

The Oxford Companion to Philosophy puts it this way:

"Humanism is an appeal to reason, in contrast to revelation or religious authority as a means of finding out about the natural world and destiny of man, and also giving a grounding for morality... Humanist ethics is also distinguished by placing the end of moral action in the welfare of humanity rather than in fulfilling the will of God."

Anything that blatantly goes against the "will of God" is demonic!

What about the New Age movement? The New Age movement spread through the occult and metaphysical religious communities in the 1970s and 1980s. It looked forward to a "new age" of love and light and offered a foretaste of the coming era (or period in time) through personal transformation and healing. The movement's strongest supporters were loyal followers of a modern religious perspective that was based on the acquisition of mystical knowledge, which has been popular in the West since the 2nd century AD.

New Age includes ritual magic and Freemasonry. Many traditional occult practices like *'tarot reading, astrology, yoga, and other meditation techniques, and mediumship,* were merged into the movement as tools to assist personal transformation. New academic disciplines that study various states of consciousness encouraged the belief that consciousness-altering practices (ancient Zen meditation) could be practiced apart from the particular contexts in which they originated. Transformative tools like channelling and the use of crystals were identified with the New Age movement as it peaked in the 1980s. Many New Agers discovered their psychic abilities and became known as channels. Either consciously, or in a trance, they claimed to establish direct interaction with various paranormal or extra-terrestrial entities who spoke through them on a wide range of philosophical, spiritual, and psychological topics. Some of the beings who "spoke" through channels became popular teachers themselves, and some of these more popular leaders founded new organizations.

As with Humanism, New Age is firmly rooted in devilish practices. What makes New Age more dangerous is the fact that it masquerades as a wholesome spiritual option to mainstream religion. However, it is void of any power to transform a person permanently because true and lasting transformation can only take place on the inside (under the guidance of the Holy Spirit). 1 John 4:4 says, *"He who is in you is greater than he who is in the world."* The spirit of the world is no match for the Holy Spirit! However, if we allow this spirit into our churches it will draw people away like sheep to the slaughter. John 10:10 warns us, *"For the thief does not come except to steal, and to kill, and to destroy."*

Let us now examine some of the various personas the "spirit of the world" takes on.

- **The spirit of greed.** Many people have allowed greed to grow into more than a selfish attitude. It is more prevalent in the area of finances than anywhere else. People that are governed by this spirit will often change character when money is around. The Bible tells us that the *love* of money is the root of all evil (1 Timothy 6:10). People driven by a spirit of greed love anything that will gratify their carnal desires – and they can never get enough of it!

- **The spirit of lust.** Covetousness (or lust) is encouraged and promoted in today's society. Sex and possessions are pursued by the majority of our population, and most restraints have been removed. James 1:14 tells us, *"But each one is tempted when he is drawn away by his own desires (lusts) and enticed."* Have you noticed how temptation is never addressed, because in the minds of many it doesn't exist. It is perfectly normal to be enticed by carnal and lustful desires (and to covet what you don't have). After all, why curb yourself when the media is heavily promoting everything that feeds the flesh? When someone has a lustful spirit you will probably notice it when he or she wants something, or more of something.

- **The spirit of perversion.** The spirit of perversion rises out of the heart. Homosexuality, lesbianism, adultery and all forms of fornication are heart issues. If you are a practicing homosexual, no matter how much you defend your lifestyle, you have a serious heart issue. Somehow the enemy was able to plant the seed in your heart that changed who you really are.

  Proverbs 4:23 says, *"Keep your heart with all diligence, for out of it are the issues of life."* In the negative... If you do not guard your heart with all diligence, out of it will flow the corrupted issues of life, and you will end up in a cesspool of sin and debauchery. The spirit of perversion resembles the cult of Baal worship, which caused ancient Israel to backslide constantly. In the New Testament, it is associated with Jezebel, the priestess of Baal, and it manifests to lead people into idolatry and immorality (Revelation 2:20). It is so important that we discern this spirit in our schools, workplace and churches.

For that is the only way we can protect our children, and the vulnerable, from paedophiles and sexual predators.

We must constantly remind ourselves that the main emphasis of the gift of the Discerning of Spirits is to "expose the works of the devil." As we do, we need to pray that the Spirit of God continues to increase through the operation of this *gift* in our homes, our schools, our workplaces and our churches. Let us distinguish that which is real (or true) from that which is false or fictitious. Let us expose the "look-alikes." Those spiritual things that appear to be the same as God, but are not. Let us shed light on all deceitful, dishonest, sinful and perverted opinions and practices. Yes, let us bring judgement on the workings of evil, and make an open show of them!

Having disarmed principalities and powers, He made a public spectacle of them, triumphing over them in it.

Colossians 2:15

10

The Gift of Tongues

The Gift of Tongues is an ability given spontaneously by the Holy Spirit to an individual to speak in a language unknown to the speaker.

The Gift of Tongues was instrumental in convincing me that my born-again experience is real. Before coming to Christ, I was very sceptical, disinterested, and suspicious of religious practices. So, it would take a Damascus Road encounter to turn me around. Growing up, I attended the Greek Orthodox church, where the priest spoke in ancient Greek. Consequently, I had never heard the Word of God and never read any of the Bible. Yet, God had a plan for my life, and He knew exactly how to reach out and connect with me in a way that He could secure my future. Here is my testimony...

I came to England as a musician in my teens, and it was over a decade before I travelled back to South Africa to visit family and friends. Immediately on arriving, my sister invited me to church. Not wanting to offend her, I reluctantly said yes. Sunday came and there I was in a Pentecostal church for the first time. The music was not to my taste, and the people were far too friendly. Anyway, I knew the church service wouldn't take long, so I wasn't that concerned. However, when the minister delivered his message, I started to become very suspicious.

You see... I am an "odds" person. I can accurately work out the odds on most things, and the odds were, "he was saying what he was saying" because I had been set up. My sister, or someone else who knew me, must have told this man about me. As a result, I was even more guarded and decided to mentally switch off – not engaging in anything that was being said. My defence barriers were up, and I thought nothing could penetrate them, but I was wrong! During the appeal, at the end of the service, something came over me and I began to weep uncontrollably. Now, these weren't tears of pain or grief. It felt as if I had just been filled with God's love and it was beginning to flow out of me. My immediate thought was, "Chris you've lived on the edge for far too long and now you have flipped." The next thought to follow was, "Well, if this is insanity then it's pretty cool." I had this lovely velvety feeling inside, and all my fears and anxieties had just disappeared. Wow! What a lovely experience!

Next, I found myself walking out to the front of the church, without even thinking! There I was standing on my own in the front of the church, not knowing what to expect next. Someone came down from the podium to pray for me. I now know that this person was Rodney Howard-Browne. He laid his hands on me, and this is what followed... I started to speak in another language. A language that was completely foreign to me. It was flowing like a river and it was fluent! My immediate thought was, "Chris, now you've really flipped!" Again, there was a supernatural peace that accompanied this experience. Fortunately, on my way out, someone gave me a little booklet called "Tongues." That night, I learnt all about the Gift of Tongues. My journey with the Lord had started with a truly supernatural experience, and what an incredible journey it's been! That day, I was "fast-tracked" into God's kingdom and the Word of Faith teaching, and have never doubted it.

What has never ceased to astound me concerning this unique occasion, was how God met me "where I was!" He knew exactly how to touch my heart and exactly what it would take to convince me *that my spiritual experience was real. Firstly, He met me at odds I couldn't fathom! Then, He made sure I would never doubt the Gift of Tongues. You see, as a proficient musician, I could probably mimic any sounds I heard. So, if I had heard "tongues" before being filled with the Holy Spirit, I may have doubted its authenticity. However, the way God planned that day, He made sure every door of doubt and unbelief was tightly sealed. The Gift of Tongues was unquestionably (for me) an important part of becoming a Christian.*

Isn't it odd how the human mind tries to fathom the things of God? Even though, *His thoughts are not our thoughts, and His ways not our ways* (Isaiah 55:8)! We must accept that realm in which the Gift of Tongues operates is not the human mind. The mind is primarily a spectator to the events, and it neither frames the utterances nor does it premeditate or arrange them. When used in private, the Gift of Tongues is for personal edification. When spoken in public, it should be for the profit (or good) of all those listening. Yet, what about Tongues in the Old Testament? Is there any reference to this *gift*, and has the human mind (in the form of ancient languages) anything to do with it?

Many believers tend to leave out the Old Testament when they are searching for Bible "truth," and yet the Old testament is part of the everlasting gospel of Christ Jesus. So, we cannot fully understand Bible truths unless we also consider what the Old Testament has to say. Speaking in tongues is no exception! Right from the start, in the book of Genesis (*chapter 10; verses 20, 31*), we will find the word "tongues" mentioned, but it simply means languages. People speaking in their own tongues were basically speaking in the language of their land.

Clearly, before Babel, all people on the earth spoke the same tongue (language), so there wasn't any problem communicating with each other. However, this did cause a problem with God, because His creation got together and started doing inconceivable things. Things that would get them to act like god's. Yes, they decided to build cities for themselves to inhabit, and also a great tower (Genesis 11:5-7). Instead of dwelling in the beautiful land God had provided, they made their own plans. Can you see why God had to act? He decided to confuse their tongue (language) so that they were unable to communicate with each other. As a result, the building of the great tower had to stop, and mankind became scattered across the earth amongst people of their own *tongue* (speech), and in their own territories.

There can be no misunderstanding about the word tongue in the Old Testament. It simply means *speaking* in the language of the nation you are from. That is, the tongues (languages) that God gave mankind after the Tower of Babel. So, if you applied this to the Gift of Tongues in the New Testament, what do you think it would mean? Does it not mean that God would give His people the *gift* of speaking in other languages in order to communicate with different nations (in their own tongue)? With one intention, and that is, to spread the gospel message of Jesus Christ. And that was undeniably demonstrated on the Day of Pentecost.

> Acts 2:1-4 *"...And when the day of Pentecost was fully come, they were all with one accord in one place. And suddenly there came a sound from heaven as of a rushing mighty wind, and it filled all the house where they were sitting. And there appeared unto them cloven tongues like as of fire, and it sat upon each of them. And they were all filled with the Holy Ghost, and began to speak with other tongues, as the Spirit gave them utterance."*

> Also, Acts 2:5-11 *"...And there were dwelling in Jerusalem Jews, devout men, from every nation under heaven. And when this sound occurred, the multitude came together, and were confused, because everyone heard them speak in his own language. Then they were all amazed and marvelled, saying to one another, "Look, are not all these who speak Galileans? And how is it that we hear, each in our own language in which we were born? Parthians and Medes and Elamites, those dwelling in Mesopotamia, Judea and Cappadocia, Pontus and Asia, Phrygia and Pamphylia, Egypt and the parts of Libya adjoining Cyrene, visitors from Rome, both Jews and*

proselytes, Cretans and Arabs—we hear them speaking in our
own tongues the wonderful works of God."

We can clearly see that the purpose of the Gift of Tongues (in this setting), was for the people from other nations, who spoke in different languages (tongues), to hear the good news of the Gospel of Jesus Christ. The Gift of Tongues was given to the disciples in the upper room on the day of Pentecost, and they were just speaking as they normally would. Yet the Holy Spirit had equipped them with a supernatural ability to speak in the various languages of the people listening. Was the Gift of Tongues given to anyone else in the New Testament? The answer is "yes," the Holy Spirit fell upon many others, enabling them to speak in *tongues* (other languages) and bring glory to God by spreading the gospel message.

> Acts 10:44-46... *"While Peter was still speaking these words, the Holy Spirit fell upon all those who heard the word. And those of the circumcision who believed were astonished, as many as came with Peter, because the gift of the Holy Spirit had been poured out on the Gentiles also. **For they heard them speak with tongues and magnify God."***

Therefore, there is a clear distinction between "speaking in tongues", as demonstrated in the scriptures above, and the Gift of Tongues mentioned by the apostle Paul in 1 Corinthians 14. However, first, I would like to clarify another point. We often refer to the Baptism of the Holy Spirit as being evidenced by speaking in tongues. I'm not sure that this is actually correct. So, let's closely examine the verses in Acts which refer to this.

> *He (Jesus) commanded them not to depart from Jerusalem, but to wait for the Promise of the Father, "which," He said, "you have heard from Me; for John truly **baptized** with water, but you shall be **baptized with the Holy Spirit** not many days from now" (Acts 1:4-5)... But you shall receive **power** when the Holy Spirit has **come upon you**; and you shall be witnesses to Me in Jerusalem, and in all Judea and Samaria, and to the end of the earth" (verse 8).*

Observe, *baptism* always represents an "immersion" and cannot be performed without it. For, John truly baptised with water - "full immersion in water." Therefore, for the baptism of the Holy Spirit to be evidenced by "speaking in tongues", there would have to be an immersion of sorts. Correct? Let's move on to the Day of Pentecost and see what transpired in the upper room...

> *"And suddenly there came a sound from heaven, as of a rushing mighty wind, and it filled the whole house where they were sitting. Then there appeared to them divided tongues, as of fire, and one sat upon each of them. And they were all **filled with the Holy Spirit and began to speak with other tongues**, as the Spirit gave them utterance"* (Acts 2:2-4).

Here, we see two distinct happenings. (1) *"Divided tongues, as of fire, sat on each one of them."* (2) *"They were all **filled** with the Holy Spirit and began to speak in other tongues."*

Infilling and immersion are totally different! Therefore, we can safely say that "speaking in tongues" was a direct result of being *"filled with the Holy Spirit."* So, what can we conclude from this? The answer comes out of the mouth of Jesus in the previous chapter... Jesus spoke about being baptised with the Holy Spirit and power coming upon them (Acts 1:5, 8). Implying that a baptism of **fire** would bring **power** from above! Notice, there is no mention of an "infilling." No mention of being **filled** with the Holy Spirit! Only a baptism with the Holy Spirit (immersion in the Holy Spirit). I am convinced that being baptised with the Holy Spirit is evidenced by **power** coming upon a believer, and not by speaking in *tongues.*

Look again at what the scripture says... *"Then there appeared to them divided tongues, as of fire, and one sat upon each of them. And they were all **filled with the Holy Spirit and began to speak with other tongues**, as the Spirit gave them utterance."* Jesus could have easily said, "And you will receive power when the Holy Spirit has filled you", but, no, He said, "You will receive power when the Holy Spirit has *come upon you*" – which is what happened here! Hence, Tongues is evidence that we are "filled" with the Holy Spirit and not baptised in the Holy Spirit. Another truth, to support this view, is the fact that "tongues, as of fire" came upon them. Fire represents "power," and tongues, in this context, is what the fire of God looked like as it manifested ("as of fire"). In other words, when the **power** of God (in the form of the Holy Spirit) divided and came to rest on each person, it resembled "tongues of fire." The result being that they all received power, when the Holy Spirit came (a full immersion), and thereafter, they were *filled* with the Holy Spirit – with the evidence of speaking in other tongues. We all need to be both baptised in the Holy Spirit (fully immersed) and filled **with** the Holy Spirit!

Let us now move on to the Gift of Tongues as described by the apostle Paul in 1 Corinthians 14 – which is different from the Gift of Tongues (speaking in other languages) mentioned in Acts 2.

I like what Kenneth Hagin says: *"This utterance, Gift of Tongues, is an important gift in that tongues is the door to the supernatural." Tongues are not the only door to communion with God, but they are a door that is always open and inviting. Tongues are supernatural in their qualities and give a depth of prayer and worship that charismatic believers find to be priceless."*

1 Corinthians 14:6-11 explains that the Gift of Tongues has four applications when used for public ministry.

> *"But now, brethren, if I come to you speaking with tongues, what shall I profit you unless I speak to you either by* **revelation**, *by* **knowledge**, *by* **prophesying**, *or by* **teaching**? *Even things without life, whether flute or harp, when they make a sound, unless they make a distinction in the sounds, how will it be known what is piped or played? For if the trumpet makes an uncertain sound, who will prepare himself for battle? So likewise you, unless you utter by the tongue words easy to understand, how will it be known what is spoken? For you will be speaking into the air. There are, it may be, so many kinds of languages in the world, and none of them is without significance. Therefore, if I do not know the meaning of the language, I shall be a foreigner to him who speaks and he who speaks will be a foreigner to me ."*

Here are the four applications of this *gift* in a public gathering:

1. to provide **revelation** concerning God's Word;

2. to give **knowledge** and understanding from God;

3. to **declare** God's message to the people (prophesying);

4. to **teach** and instruct in reference to the Word of God;

We must remember that the emphasis is always on the needs of the hearer and not the needs of the speaker. What's more, even if the tongue is delivered in a clear and a meaningful language, if that *language* is not known by those listening, then there has been no communication. Nothing has been accomplished! Also, no one present has benefited or been built up. So, if there's been no **revelation** from God, no **knowledge** imparted, no **prophecy** made, no **instruction** accomplished - the gift is useless.

Tongues will certainly have some attraction for many people. However, unless we are taught correctly, the tongue spoken, or message given, is futile. In this verse, Paul speaks of *revelation*, knowledge, prophecy and instruction. Revelation played a very important role in the early church. In Galatians 2:2, we see how Paul "by revelation" went up to Jerusalem to consult with the apostles of the church (Galatians 2:2). It was by divine revelation that Paul and Barnabas were sent on their First Missionary Journey (Acts 13:1-3). It was also by divine revelation that Paul and Silas were sent into the area that would become Europe (Acts 16:6-10). Subsequently, it was by revelation knowledge that the Gospel came to us all.

The Gift of Speaking in Tongues must fully line up with, and be measured against, the infallible Word of God (as with the Gift of Prophecy). That is why it needs to be interpreted. If we do not know what is being said, how can we determine whether the message is in agreement with God's Word or not! *Verse 9* tells us that without interpretation of the tongues, with words that are easily understood, there is no communication. Therefore, we will be unsuccessful in trying to communicate God's message to anyone unless they fully understand what we are saying. If they do not comprehend what we are saying, the result will be frustration and disengagement.

Verses 16-17 affirm that without being able to fully comprehend the message, the listener is not built up.

> *"Therefore let him who speaks in a tongue pray that he may interpret. For if I pray in a tongue, my spirit prays, but my understanding is unfruitful. What is the conclusion then? I will pray with the spirit, and I will also pray with the understanding. I will sing with the spirit, and I will also sing with the understanding. Otherwise, if you bless with the spirit, how will he who occupies the place of the uninformed say "Amen" at your giving of thanks, since he does not understand what you say? For you indeed give thanks well, but the other is not* **edified**.*"*

Paul reiterates this in 1 Corinthians 14:18, *"I thank my God I speak with tongues more than you all; yet in the church I would rather speak five words with my understanding, that I may* **teach** *others also, than ten thousand words in a tongue."* Paul wrote about the superiority of prophecy over tongues, yet he began by saying that he wished all believers spoke in tongues and then qualified this wish by stating "publicly spoken tongues" ought to be interpreted. That is because, when interpreted, they will edify the body of Christ. 1 Corinthians 15:5, *"I wish you all spoke with tongues, but even more that you prophesied; for he who prophesies is greater than he who speaks with tongues, unless indeed he* **interprets**, *that the church may receive* **edification**.*"* When it comes to public speaking in tongues, the emphasis is always on the hearer and not on the speaker. The reason being... the hearer must receive edification at all times!

I would now like to examine the Biblical basis for Speaking in Tongues in **Private**. Praying in tongues in private is an incredibly useful tool for every believer. In fact, it is fundamental to living the super-abundant life that Jesus secured for us. It also helps us to make intercession on behalf of others. So, let's see what the Bible says about this subject...

First, Jesus Himself stated that speaking in tongues would be practiced. He told the eleven that one of the signs which would be visible among those who believe is that, *"they will speak with new tongues"* (Mark 16:17). No matter how one theologically analyses this statement by Jesus, we would have to conclude that Jesus' statement is a definite affirmation of speaking in tongues. He did not elaborate, give details, qualify his statement, define tongues, or distinguish between public or private tongues, but He did make it clear that it would happen. Neither did Jesus say whether it would be a one-time occurrence among distinct groups of Christians or an ongoing experience among individual believers. Yet, what He did state is this, *"included among those who call on His Name will be those who speak with new tongues."*

The apostle Paul affirmed speaking in tongues as an act of private devotion. We find strong support for diversity in tongues in 1 Corinthians 12. *"Different kinds of tongues"* are mentioned as being manifest by the Holy Spirit and *"given to each one for the profit of all"* (verse 7). Paul then lists several gifts (verse 8-10), which includes *"different kinds of tongues."* In Chapter 14, Paul admonishes the church at Corinth to *"pursue love, and desire spiritual gifts, but especially that you may prophesy."* Although Paul spends the remainder of the chapter contrasting the Gift of Prophecy with the Gift of Tongues, Paul does not forbid speaking in tongues - publicly or privately.

In spite of many attempts to explain this verse away, Paul is clear and unmistakable in 1 Corinthians 14:2, *"For he who speaks in a tongue does not speak to men but to God, for no one understands him; however, in the spirit he speaks mysteries."* Speaking to God is the most fundamental definition of prayer. Paul further explains that because a believer is speaking to God and not man (in prayer), *"no one understands him."*

The reason that no one understands him is because, *"in the spirit he speaks mysteries."* The prayer that Paul is describing here has to be done privately, since he later forbids this type of prayer during corporate worship without interpretation (verses 27-28).

Paul reveals that anyone who speaks in tongues (in this manner) *"edifies himself."* The fact that he edifies himself is yet another indication that this type of praying in tongues was to be done privately. Prophecy, by nature, is public or at least, focused on another person. But this type of prayer is private and is directed to God alone. The intrinsic nature of private prayer is *self-edification*, which results in God's glorification. Jude taught that when believers *"pray in the Spirit,"* they build themselves up (Jude 20). When a believer builds himself up by praying in the Spirit, he/she is then better equipped to *"fight the good fight of faith"* and *"earnestly contend for the faith."* Furthermore, built-up believers can then strengthen and encourage other believers. As a result, someone who prays in the Spirit at all times, and edifies himself, can also build up the church.

Our private prayers often take on a different character than our public prayers. Jesus told us to go and pray in a secret place. In that secluded place, our prayers are often expressed with words we understand. Though, they can also be expressed with words we do not understand and sometimes with no words at all. One of my favourite passages is Romans 8:26-27,

> *"Likewise the Spirit also helps in our weaknesses. For we do not know what we should pray for as we ought, but the Spirit Himself makes intercession for us with groanings which cannot be uttered. Now He who searches the hearts knows what the mind of the Spirit is, because He makes intercession for the saints according to the will of God."*

Douglas Moo (*The Epistle to the Romans* [Eerdmans], p. 526) summarizes Paul's thought in these verses:

> Paul is revealing this truth... *that our failure to know God's will and consequent inability to petition God specifically and assuredly is met by God's Spirit, who himself expresses to God those intercessory petitions that perfectly match the will of God. When we do not know what to pray for—yes, even when we pray for things that are not best for us—we need not despair, for we can depend on the Spirit's ministry of perfect intercession "on our behalf."*

Paul's overall objective is clear. He wants to encourage us, especially when we are being held back by our own weakness (human frailties), through the knowledge that the Holy Spirit is praying for us. Even though we do not know how to pray as we should, we must be encouraged to keep on praying anyway. However, there are a number of details in these verses that may be a little difficult to comprehend. The first, is to determine what "in the same way" refers to. Some commentators connect it to the theme of "groaning." In Romans 8:22, the whole of creation groans; in Romans 8:23, we ourselves groan as we wait for the completion of our adoption as God's children. So, *"in the same way,"* the Holy Spirit *"intercedes for us with groanings too deep for words."* The simple truth is, Paul wants us to feel encouraged by the fact that the Spirit is praying for us, and that way, we will be encouraged to keep praying.

MacLaren's Expositions commentary states...

> *Pentecost was a transitory sign of a perpetual gift. The tongues of fire and the rushing mighty wind, which were at first the most conspicuous results of the gifts of the Spirit, tongues, and prophecies, and gifts of healing, which were to the early Church itself and to onlookers palpable demonstrations of an indwelling power, were little more lasting than the fire and the wind. Does anything remain?*

> *This whole great chapter is Paul's triumphant answer to such a question. The Spirit of God dwells in every believer as the source of his true life, is for him 'the Spirit of adoption' and witnesses with his spirit that he is a child of God, and a joint-heir with Christ. Not only does that Spirit co-operate with the human spirit in this witness-bearing, but the verse, of which our text is a part, points to another form of co-operation: for the word rendered in the earlier part of the verse 'helps' in the original suggests more distinctly that the Spirit of God in His intercession for us works in association with us.*

That means "groanings" represent Spirit induced sounds, which flow out of our inner-being. Such groans/longings can only manifest when we are praying in the Spirit. They are our own divinely-inspired utterances, which are understood only by the Spirit and God Himself. Yet, they still strengthen and build us up in times of need. The assurance we get from these verses is truly inspiring. For when we do not know how to pray as we ought, we have confidence in the fact that the Holy Spirit will cooperate with us in order to make sure we pray according to the perfect will of God. When we do, we are guaranteed to have our prayers and petitions answered.

Observe, our failure to know God's will and inability to petition Him correctly, is replaced by God's Spirit (as we pray in the Spirit) - who Himself expresses to God those intercessory requests that perfectly match the will of God. I have so often prayed in tongues in private, only to discover that inconceivable supernatural interventions have taken place because of my prayers. This could only have come about through the Holy Spirit making intercession on my behalf – according to the will of God! There were times when I have been compelled to pray in the Spirit (in tongues), without knowing why or what I am praying for.

Nevertheless, I know that my prayers are needed (and vital) even if they are not necessarily for me. Since, there may be someone on the other side of the world that is in imminent danger, and my prayers can release the power of God to deliver them from destruction. In such 'life and death' situations, I know that I'm praying the perfect will of God. Consequently, I have the self-assurance that God will hear, and He will answer!

Now, there may be times in all our lives when prayer is difficult. We may even be in situations where prayer is almost impossible. I'm sure you can think of a time when you wanted to pray, but the adverse circumstances have left you speechless. Regardless of your feelings, the promise in these two verses should bring much comfort. Remember, this is not simply a passage to turn to when our prayer life is not quite what we would like it to be. For, even when we feel like our prayer life is going well, we still need the Holy Spirit to intercede for us (or others). We still need "God's perfect will" to be implemented – for we are unlikely to know what it is!

Finally, although the groanings of the Spirit (in private prayer) are without words, they are not meaningless. So, be encouraged! Pray in the Spirit at all times! *"Praying always with all prayer and supplication in the Spirit, being watchful to this end with all perseverance and supplication for all the saints"* (Ephesians 6:18).

11

The Gift of Interpretation of Tongues

"Wherefore, let him who speaks with an unknown tongue (λαλῶν γλώσσῃ) pray (προσευχέσθω) that he may interpret"

The Gift of Interpretation of Tongues is as supernatural as the Gift of Tongues. However, it is the only *gift* of the Holy Spirit that is totally reliant on another *gift* for it to operate. The Interpretation of Tongues cannot function unless the Gift of Tongues has first communicated a message. This gift is, therefore, the least of all the utterance *gifts*.

Interpretation of Tongues provides supernatural clarification, by the Holy Spirit, concerning the general meaning of an utterance delivered in tongues. It's not a translation of tongues - it's an interpretation of tongues! To translate a message would mean it was "word for word," or as near to an exact meaning as likely. However, to interpret a message is to paraphrase its meaning or to bring out the essence of it. Therefore, interpretation of a tongue is never verbatim (letter-perfect) - it may be shorter or longer, as the Holy Spirit leads.

We must also realize that our personalities and character traits will be come through as we interpret a tongue. Those of us who are very intellectual will more than likely use elaborate words when bringing a message from God. Those of us who are more practical, will tend to keep the messages simple and to the point. The Holy Spirit, working through us, does not suddenly change our character when operating His gifts.

God has supernaturally equipped every one of us with different personalities, qualities and character traits that identify who we are in His family. As with all our families, not everyone has the same attributes. Our personalities will be both seen and heard when we interpret a message from the Lord. If you are very demonstrative when you talk, you will be demonstrative when delivering a word from the Lord. If you are very loud and ablaze for Jesus, this will also be evident in the message. If you are a detail type of person, the interpretation may be longer than the tongue because you are focusing on the smallest details so that the listeners understand more fully. So, the final interpretation will depend upon who the Holy Spirit has decided to use. Note, it won't change the meaning of the message, because it's Spirit inspired. However, the expression will be different based on the character of the vessel being used.

The main purpose of this *gift* is to make the Gift of Tongues understandable and logical to the hearer, in order for the church to be edified (built up). In 1 Corinthians 14:12 the apostle Paul says, *"Even so you, since you are zealous for spiritual gifts, let it be for the edification of the church that you seek to excel."* All the *gifts* of the Holy Spirit are to be used to bring edification, comfort and encouragement to the Body of Christ. They are not to draw attention to those being used for the manifestation of the *gift*. The Gifts of the Holy Spirit are not "gifts of the church" because they are totally exclusive to God's Spirit.

I cannot stress enough the importance for Christians to learn how to be receptive and sensitive to the moving of God's Spirit. I believe our response levels grow and mature when we spend quality time in God's presence, communing with Him on a daily basis. Likewise, when our sensitivity levels surge and we become openly receptive, we are quick to follow God's promptings and obey His instructions. Consequently, when He directs us to do something different, something that was not planned, we are poised to move with the Spirit. We won't become frustrated or feel unfulfilled when the Holy Spirit starts to minister. Instead, we will be content with the knowledge that God has a specific plan for that day and for that particular group of people. I have learnt to accept that the Holy Spirit never operates in exactly the same way in any given situation. He is always fresh and original in His actions. After all, He is the Spirit of creativity!

We have examined Interpretation of Tongues during a public assembly (ἐκκλησία), but what about Interpretation of Tongues in our personal prayer time? First, we must agree that praying in tongues is primarily an "offering to God," so it shouldn't need interpretation. That said, how can we be edified if we do not know what is being spoken? The answer is... by taking comfort in the knowledge that when we pray in the Spirit we are praying according to the will of God. This pleases Him. Therefore, if I know God is pleased with me, I always feel encouraged and built-up.

Lastly, we need to know what the difference is between praying in the Spirit and praying in tongues? The best way to find out is to examine the scripture verses that refer to this subject.

Here are three that clearly mention praying in, or with, the Holy Spirit:

- 1 Corinthians 14:15, *"What is the conclusion then? I will pray **with the spirit**, and I will also pray with the understanding. I will sing with the spirit, and I will also sing with the understanding."*

- Ephesians 6:18, *"...praying always with all prayer and supplication **in the Spirit**, being watchful to this end with all perseverance and supplication for all the saints."*

- Jude 20, *"But you, beloved, building yourselves up on your most holy faith, praying **in the Holy Spirit**."*

Let's compare 1 Corinthians 14:15 to Ephesians 6:18 and Jude 20. The first thing we notice is that in the first scripture, for the word spirit, the "s" is not in capitals. Yet, it is in the other two. So, are these verses referring to two different experiences? Let's look at the first reference in a little more detail. In 1 Corinthians 14:15, Paul is definitely talking about praying in *tongues* since that is the context in which it was written. Yet, because the word "spirit" is not in capitals it cannot be referring to the Holy Spirit (as with the other two verses). Hence, Paul can only be citing a person praying with his/her spirit, and not the Holy Spirit. Notice also that 1 Corinthians uses the phrase *"with the spirit,"* as opposed to *"in the Spirit,"* which is mentioned in the other two references. I believe Paul is writing about a person praying out of his or her own spirit, which is probably not limited to any recognised language. I like how the Amplified Bible puts it:

"Then what am I to do? I will pray with my spirit [by the Holy Spirit that is within me], but I will also pray [intelligently] with my mind and understanding;..."

Paul says that he will pray with his spirit, as well as being led by the Holy Spirit that dwells within him. The process of being *"led by the Spirit of God"* can definitely result in praying in tongues. I have often felt that the Spirit is leading me to pray in tongues, and this urgency comes from within and not from my intellect or any outside influences. If you are a son or daughter of God, you should never underestimate the magnitude of being led by God's Spirit. *"For those who are (continually) led by the Spirit of God are children of God."* (Romans 8:14).

Observing the other two passages (Ephesians 6:18 and Jude 20), we find the phrase *"pray in the Spirit."* This refers to the realm where our prayers are positioned. It means, when we are "in" the Holy Spirit, we are always guided "by" the Holy Spirit. The process for praying "in" the Spirit involves our spirit because God's Spirit communicates to and through our spirit. Hence, in order to be led by the Holy Spirit and pray accordingly, we must be praying with our spirit's involvement and full cooperation (John 4:23-24). We could, therefore, say that *"praying in the Spirit"* is referring to prayers that are Holy Spirit inspired – whether this is in a public forum or a private prayer-room. Furthermore, it may at times include tongues and interpretation of tongues.

Praying in the Spirit is an inspired prayer that is instigated solely by God's Spirit and then manifests 'when' and 'how' He may choose. Note, we can pray from our own spirit and these prayers may still be legitimate. However, they will not have the power to change situations or the power to edify and strengthen us. Many times we feel led to pray for things we want, or need, or for the needs of others. Yet, there will be times when God wants us to use the power of prayer to accomplish His will in a specific and unique situation. That is when praying in tongues is vital!

Romans 8:26, *"Likewise the Spirit also helps in our weaknesses. For we do not know what we should pray for as we ought, but the Spirit Himself makes intercession for us with groanings which cannot be uttered."*

Praying "in" the Spirit and praying "with" the spirit are separate experiences, even though they're related to each other. Praying "in" the Spirit encompasses many types of prayers – including praying in tongues. It guarantees that our prayers, when led by the Holy Spirit, carry the power of the Holy Spirit (and the favour of God). However, praying "with" the spirit simply means that we are praying with our spirit and not our intellect. This does not mean that praying with the mind is a bad thing (1 Corinthians 14:15), but, rather, that the particular prayer we present to God, may or may not be inspired or directed by the Holy Spirit. When we decide to pray with the spirit, it will not necessarily be consistent with praying in tongues. Therefore, there won't be the requirement to pray for an interpretation.

John 4:23-24, *"But the hour is coming, and now is, when the true worshipers will worship the Father in spirit and truth; for the Father is seeking such to worship Him. God is Spirit, and those who worship Him must worship in spirit and truth."*

Our prayers, as with our worship, must fully engage our spirit - because God is Spirit. Praying with our spirit is when we truly communicate to God what is held deep in our heart. Then, when our prayers are directed or led by the Holy Spirit, praying in the Spirit becomes even more effective, with often miraculous results. Yet, whichever way we choose to pray, whether in the Spirit or with the spirit, we must remember that whatever we present to God in prayer (with a pure heart), He receives and then responds with blessings.

Again, we must not feel under pressure to pray in any particular way. However, when we do pray in tongues, and it is in a public place, we should pray for the interpretation. Also, when we are praying in tongues privately, we should ask God whether we need the interpretation to our prayers (for any reason). If we do need to know what it is we are praying (in the Spirit), the Holy Spirit will provide the interpretation. Nevertheless, we will always be blessed!

I spend a lot of time praying in tongues, without any expectation to receive an interpretation. I pray *"in the Spirit"* while driving the car, or meditating on matters that need urgent attention, or when I feel my faith needs to be activated. Most of all, I pray in tongues (*in the Spirit*) during corporate worship (before I am about to preach/teach). It is incredible how the Holy Spirit prepares and strengthens us for service – as we pray in tongues. Without Him, I am sure we would really struggle. So, praise the Lord for His faithfulness!

Finally, we should be aware that the interpretation of a tongue (in the church) is not always given by the individual who has spoken the tongue. It can come through someone else, or even more than one person. However, it must always be done in order. The apostle Paul was so concerned that the Gifts of the Holy Spirit were being abused (and especially tongues), he chose to write to the church in Corinth and lay down some guidelines.

The next chapter details some of the rules he implemented.

12

Policies and Procedures

In 1 Corinthians 14:27-28, Paul provides guidelines on how tongues should be treated in a corporate worship service. He writes,

> *"If anyone speaks in a tongue, it should be by two or at the most three, and each in turn, and one must interpret; but if there is no interpreter, he must keep silent in the church; and let him speak to himself and to God."*

Here are Paul's rules for speaking in tongues (according to the scripture above):

- No more than three, preferably two, should speak in tongues in a given service.

- Only one person should speak in tongues at a time.

- No one should speak unless an interpreter is present. Before one speaks in a tongue he must know there is an interpreter available - not just assume there is one.

After providing rules and procedures on tongues, Paul offers some restrictions on prophecy.

In verses 29-32, Paul writes, *"Let two or three prophets speak, and let the others pass judgment. But if a revelation is made to another who is seated, the first one must keep silent. For you can all prophesy one by one, so that all may learn and all may be exhorted; and the spirits of prophets are subject to prophets."*

Paul's instructions on prophecy are as follows:

- Limit prophesying to two or three speakers. Keep it short as not to exasperate the listeners.

- The church is to weigh carefully what is being said. The Greek word used here means "to evaluate carefully."

- One prophecy at a time. Prophesying is to be done in turn. If one person desires to speak, and he is authorised by the leaders, he or she should be given the opportunity.

Paul ends this section by sharing a key principle to bear in mind: *"God is not a God of confusion but of peace."* Paul wants these procedures (in a church setting) not to be disruptive but to be orderly. He has already stated one reason for this opinion, namely, that unbelievers will be turned off if there is chaos due to a free-for-all attitude. Orderly worship is a reflection of the intrinsic character of God. God is a God of order!

Paul then addresses another important directive, and that is: *"Respect God-ordained authority"* (verses 33-40). In this section, Paul provides a number of ways we can respect the authority that God has put in place over us. He begins with a controversial subject. Paul brings up the issue of women in ministry, and their role in the church. What we must understand is that this passage is not an absolute denial to women having a public ministry in the church (or anywhere else).

Paul clearly acknowledges that in certain situations a woman may pray or prophesy. While both men and women could prophesy (1 Corinthians 11:4-5), it's not unreasonable to suggest that husband and wife might say different or even contradictory things, and this could lead to an argument in front of the rest of the church.

Or, if a prophecy was given and the church evaluated what was said (1 Corinthians 14: 29), once again a husband and wife could end up in public disagreement as to the content of that prophecy. That's why Paul considers this to be distasteful and, therefore, aims to avoid such confrontation because it could damage the witness of the local church. I'm sure the procedures Paul has put in place were done with much wisdom, insight and sensitivity. There is no evidence that he was being chauvinistic!

In the closing verses, Paul draws this entire section to a close, and in 1 Corinthians 14:36, he writes, *"Was it from you that the word of God first went forth? Or has it come to you only?"* We would expect the answer to these two questions to be "no." However, Paul is seeking to humble the arrogant Corinthians, so he drives home the point of his argument. In 1 Corinthians 14: 37-38, in the imperative tense, Paul writes, *"If anyone thinks he is a prophet or spiritual, let him recognize that the things which I write to you are the Lord's commandment. But if anyone does not recognize this, he is not recognized."* Paul gives what can be read as a stern warning. Anyone who ignores the advice he has just given will not be recognized as a leader. Furthermore, God will ignore these individuals and accomplish His work without them. This approach definitely keeps certain people in line and deters them from misusing the *gifts*.

Paul is now ready to sum up this lengthy section. In verse 39, he writes, *"Therefore, my brethren, desire earnestly to prophesy, and do not forbid anyone to speak in tongues."* Again, we should desire prophecy and refuse to forbid speaking in tongues.

Remember, if someone present has the Gift of Interpretation, then the freedom to speak in tongues is supported. Yet, there always needs to be order when people are allowed to speak in tongues openly. Many Christians miscalculate in the extreme! Either everyone speaks in tongues or no one speaks in tongues! The whole focus of this chapter, has been to control the public use of tongues – not to stop it. In fact, the three main positive statements in the chapter are each followed by the word "but:"

- Verse 5: *"I wish you all spoke in tongues, **but**..."*

- Verse 18: *"I thank God, I speak in tongues more than you all; **but**..."*

- Verse 39: *"Do not forbid to speak in tongues, **but**..."*

In each of the above verses, the "but" introduces Paul's concerns for the church. Our public assembly must focus on the Word of God. Our services must be decent and orderly, and they should follow the biblical guidelines on tongues and interpretation of tongues.

Paul's final words in this section sum up all of his concerns: *"But all things must be done properly and in an orderly manner"* (verse 40). The word "order" is a military term for falling in rank. Paul only uses this word in one other context, and it is translated "stability or firmness." When the body of Christ functions the way it is intended, there will be a sense of stability and rigidity. The church should be seen to be established on the Rock.

I am convinced that the greatest church-growth tool is God's presence. If people experience God's presence in worship, they will come back, and they will tell their friends, and they will continually long for it. The Gifts of the Spirit are an integral part of corporate worship because they amplify God's presence in the church.

13

Spiritual Gifts and Corporate Worship

"ekklesia" (ἐκκλησία) refers to a local assembly of believers in Jesus Christ

When examining the Gifts of the Holy Spirit (1 Corinthians 12, 13,14), and their various operations, we must first acknowledge the fact that they are intended to manifest during our corporate worship (as we assemble together). That is why they benefit (edify) everyone present! Paul was writing and giving instructions to a specific church in a specific location – Corinth. It was through their misuse of the *gifts* in corporate worship that we are given insight into how God intends for them to operate. However, the setting in which the Holy Spirit initiates His *gifts* must also be fully understood. Due to God's Spirit being present in every believer, the gifts can manifest anywhere and at any time He chooses. However, according to 1 Corinthians 14:12, we should strive to excel in the *gifts* that build up and strengthen the whole church. This theme is woven into all the guidance and instruction that Paul provides throughout these chapters.

Now, let us look closely at the setting and environment which represents corporate worship. First, we must reach agreement on the meaning of worship (and where exactly it is intended to take place). The word *"ekklesia"* has been branded as some superior and unique technique for extending God's kingdom – a tool to bring about social transformation. So, let us acquire more clarity on this word... Centuries before the translation of the Old Testament, or the era of the New Testament, the word *"ekklesia"* (ἐκκλησία) was clearly characterized as a political phenomenon, repeated according to certain rules and within a certain frame-work. It referred to the assembly of full citizens, functionally rooted in the constitution of Greek democracy. An **assembly** in which fundamental political and judicial decisions were taken. However, the word *"ekklesia"* in itself does not reveal 'who' is meeting, only that a certain group has been called to assemble.

What is noteworthy, however, is that the word "ἐκκλησία" when used throughout the Greek and Hellas territories, always retained its reference to an **assembly**. The normal usage of this Greek word in New Testament times was understood to mean "those called out for a specific purpose" or a "special assembly." "Ekklesia" could therefore refer to different kinds of assemblies within the context of the words used to explain who was meeting (those attending the gathering). There is no doubt in my mind that this ancient Greek word always refers to a gathering together of people for an intended purpose. Hence, "a calling out" or "calling forth." In the context of corporate worship, it is a congregation of believers who have been "called out" with the intended purpose of worshipping God.

If we stopped here, there would be no argument or reason to differ. However, whenever God's people came together to worship there was a fundamental requirement.

That fundamental requirement was founded on a covenant that God Himself made. Right from the start, God made a covenant with His people to meet with them and dwell among them. It is because of this covenant that God's presence is among us today. The Old Testament saints felt a deep longing for the presence of God, and it is symbolised in the temple ruins. And before that, the temple itself. And before that, the ark of the covenant and the tabernacle that housed it. And even before that, the Garden of Eden. It was in response to this longing that God made a covenant in which His people play a big part. God wants to dwell (in the Hebrew "glory") among His people, but He also wants the privilege of choosing where that should take place. Exodus 25:8 confirms this, *"Then have them build me a sanctuary, that I may dwell among them."*

Initially, God chose the Tabernacle and gave Moses the exact dimensions and requirements for this meeting place (Exodus 26:16-18). The Tabernacle was a "place of dwelling." It was a sacred location where God chose to meet with His people. Yet, the Tabernacle was more than just a dwelling place, for all the components of the tabernacle were part of an intricate visual aid to illustrate God's covenant relationship with His people. Fast forward to the New Testament... has everything changed? Definitely not! For, God is the same *yesterday, today and forever* (Psalm 102:24-27; Malachi 3:6; Hebrews 13:8). Just because the Greek word "ἐκκλησία" was used to denote a gathering of God's people, doesn't mean that God Himself has ceased to fulfil His promise to "dwell" among us! As always, God's dwelling place is where His people are assembled together. In Matthew 18:20, Jesus says, *"For where two or three are gathered together in My name, I am there in the midst of them."*

Worship has, and always will be about God's presence – God dwelling in the midst of His people. This is a divine covenant!

Any examination of corporate worship must, therefore, start with a prerequisite, and that is, God only accepts worship offered within a covenant framework. Any legitimate definition of "worship" (that aspires to be Biblical) must first acknowledge that worship is a celebration of one's covenant relationship with a Holy God. The word covenant simply describes an explicit relationship between two parties, in this case, God and us. The relationship has clearly defined prerequisites and commitments. Sometimes, both parties to the covenant must keep all the commitments for the covenant to remain in force (and that is a conditional covenant), while at other times, God promises to uphold the covenant with no mention being made of the other party's responsibilities (and this is an unconditional or unilateral covenant).

Now that we have established the necessity of covenant in corporate worship, let's see how this relates to New Testament practices. In the New Testament, the presence of the Holy Spirit seals the covenant God made with His people (the worshipers) as the other party to the promise. He takes God's place as the "manifest presence of God." However, the Holy Spirit's second function in worship is the creation of a worshiping community (the "ἐκκλησία"). Biblical covenants always involve a group of people. God may redeem individuals, but His goal is the creation of a worshipping group – assembled together for that purpose. In the Old Testament, God did exactly what He had promised. He redeemed His people and then brought them together into a community of persons that inhabit the very covenant He made (Psalm 106:4; Isaiah 11:12).

It is also interesting to note that the ancient Greek word for church building is "kyriakos" (κυριακός), which is "belonging to the Lord" or "the Lord's house." This lines up perfectly with Ezekiel 43, "the Lord's dwelling place."

For Christians this experience of community becomes a reality through the Holy Spirit dwelling in each covenant member. He unites believers into a single people, the community of Christ. At one level the Spirit connects and joins the members of a local congregation together into a functioning community. At a higher level, God's Spirit unites all believers, both as individuals and communities to other Christians everywhere. He erases the separation of space and geography between each congregation. In an age when God's covenant with humanity extends beyond the Old Testament ethnic and geographic boundaries, only the Spirit makes "corporate" worship possible. Therefore, for those living in the light of the New Covenant, corporate worship (that is acceptable to God) embraces a covenant community that has been created and qualified by the Holy Spirit. This covenant community, the gathering of those called out with an intended purpose, is the "ἐκκλησία" The very place where they have chosen to worship is where you will find God's presence.

It is all about God's presence! Therefore, when we understand the principles outlined above, we get to realise that the Holy Spirit is key to acceptable corporate worship. Just as the Holy Spirit defines the covenant community and unifies its members, He empowers our participation to edify each other within that community (the church). Not only do we need the Holy Spirit to manifest the presence of God in our services, we need Him to manifest His gifts! Remember, the Gifts of the Holy Spirit serve to **magnify** the presence of God! Without the gifts, our corporate worship is without presence, purpose or power!

"But the hour is coming, and now is, when the true worshipers will worship the Father in spirit and truth; for the Father is seeking such to worship Him. God is Spirit, and those who worship Him must worship in spirit and truth"

(John 4:23-24).

14

The Voice

"As God's representative on the earth, He has given us the authority to speak for Him. When we speak under the leading of the Holy Spirit, we speak as His voice on the earth."

Barbara Wentroble

To be truly *spiritual* is to be a true worshipper. To be true worshippers, we must worship the Lord *"in spirit and in truth"* – under the inspiration and guidance of the Holy Spirit. Therefore, the Holy Spirit is fundamental to our corporate worship. Without Him, we cannot live the holy life that identifies us, qualifies us and supports our service to God. Is the Holy Spirit meant to lead our corporate worship? Yes, He leads *all* forms of worship, whether planned or unplanned, formal or casual, traditional or free-flowing. God's Spirit consistently leads through the *gifts* He has given the Church! However, does the Holy Spirit have enough freedom to function as He may desire in our churches today? Probably not! However, each week we have another opportunity to increase our sensitivity to His leading, and surrender to His gentle guidance.

For God's people, worship is the highest vocation. It's the reason we were created. It's the very purpose of our existence. Under the new covenant, the Spirit's presence is the "seal" that helps to identify those who have chosen to live God's way (through faith in Jesus Christ). The Spirit assists us in building a worshiping community, creating an earthly sanctuary of worship to the Living God. He inspired the Word of God and illuminates it with revelation to guide and direct us during our worship services.

In the process, the Holy Spirit enables the Church to display the manifold wisdom of God to principalities, powers and rules of darkness (Ephesians 3:10), which is critical to our understanding of spiritual matters. The Holy Spirit is a multifaceted expression of God's power, love and divine character. Only He can make intercession on our behalf (Romans 8:27). Only He can search and know the mind and heart of God... *"Is there anyone who can understand his own thoughts except his own inner spirit? In the same way, no one can know the thoughts of God except God's Spirit. But as it is written: 'Eye has not seen, nor ear heard, nor have entered into the heart of man the things which God has prepared for those who love Him'."* (1 Corinthians 2:11; Phillips)

Having written about His marvellous *gifts*, I have come to the conclusion that the Holy Spirit is the single most treasured connection we ought to maintain - in life and in service to God. If we are to be truly *spiritual*, we should continually nurture and cherish that relationship. After telling us He would not leave us orphaned, Jesus said,

> *"These things I have spoken to you while being present with you. But the Helper, the Holy Spirit, whom the Father will send in My name, He will teach you all things, and bring to your remembrance all things that I said to you"* (John 14:25-26).

Jesus was implying that, because He had gone to the Father, we should continue to have "relationship" with Him through the Person of the Holy Spirit.

Observe, the Helper is doing exactly what Jesus would do if He was present. He is the perfect and complete representation of Jesus Christ - just as Jesus was the perfect and complete representation of God the Father. *"Who, being the brightness of His glory and the express image of His person, and upholding all things by the word of His power"* (Hebrews 1:3). *"If you had known Me, you would have known My Father also; and from now on you know Him and have seen Him"* (John 14:7).

To continue the ministry of Jesus, the Body of Christ must be fully engaged with the Holy Spirit. Otherwise, the prophecy that Jesus made in John 14:12 can never be fulfilled, *"Most assuredly, I say to you, he who believes in Me, the works that I do he will do also; and greater works than these he will do, because I go to My Father."* The Holy Spirit brings glory to Jesus by doing the works Jesus did, however, they must now be done *through* the church. This is probably not happening to the degree Jesus prophesied, and that's because our relationship with God's Spirit is not convincing enough. The Holy Spirit is a perfect gentleman. So, unless your heart is fully in tune to His heart, He will not manifest any of His *gifts*.

In John 16:7, Jesus said, *"Nevertheless I tell you the truth. It is to your **advantage** that I go away; for if I do not go away, the Helper will not come to you; but if I depart, I will send Him to you."* Think about that... It is to our advantage, for our gain, that Jesus went to the Father! Why? If the Lord didn't leave, He couldn't send the Holy Spirit – *"the Helper will not come to you."* The question is, "Do we see this as an incredible advantage, or do we merely accept it as a free gift?" We ought to appreciate all the advantages we have gained, through the Holy Spirit's coming, every single day! For, that is the very reason why we can now live the super-abundant life that Jesus has secured for us (John 10:10).

The Holy Spirit appears 59 times in the book of Acts, and in 36 of those appearances, He is speaking. How often do we allow Him to talk to us in our corporate worship today? How much guidance are we receiving from Him during our services? As John Newton put it, "Is it really true that the very thing which the early church so depended on - the leadership of the Spirit - is irrelevant to us today?" The most common way the Holy Spirit speaks in Acts (other than through scripture), is through the Church. The Church is a divine instrument from which God sends messages. For instance, Acts 13:2 records, *"While [the church was] worshiping the Lord and fasting, the Holy Spirit said, 'Set apart for me Barnabas and Saul for the work to which I have called them.'"* God gave the church specific insight into what Saul and Barnabas were to do. Throughout his life, Paul received instructions about where to go and what to do through the members of his church, and he gave similar words of instruction to Timothy. I have found no reason to believe that God has stopped speaking through the Church.

A word of caution... If we are to receive instruction and guidance through God's Spirit, it will more than likely be *'as He manifests His gifts'*. Therefore, if we are ignorant of spiritual matters (the Gifts of the Holy Spirit), our hearing will be seriously impaired. For this reason, we must study what the Word of God says about the gifts and their various operations. We must have knowledge and understanding about what is, or is not, divinely spiritual. We cannot be led astray be erroneous teaching and soulish practices. The devil knows that if he can misdirect our corporate worship, he can keep us away from the presence of God. Always remind yourself of this fact... The main reason why God's Spirit speaks through the Church is to magnify and amplify the Voice of God. God desires to be heard in our lives and in our corporate worship services!

In Isaiah 42:14, the Lord declares, *"I have held My peace a long time, I have been still and restrained Myself. Now I will cry out like a woman in labour, I will pant and gasp at once."* This passage is referring to the "new things" that God is announcing, which are being brought to fruition (verse 9). Much of what God is expressing here concerns Him being vocal. Simply, God is crying out to be heard!

Society has muted the Voice of God and amplified the voice of the devil. However, the time has come for the Church to rectify this. We cannot allow God's voice to be smothered by political correctness and unrighteous social liberties. As we continually sing His praises, it says, *"The Lord shall go forth like a mighty man; He shall stir up His zeal like a man of war. He shall **cry out**, yes, **shout aloud**; He shall prevail against His enemies"* (verse 13).

The Lord's battle cry needs to be heard! The only way this can happen is if the Holy Spirit is permitted to magnify God in our corporate services. He must be given the privilege and freedom to manifest His "war-cry" in our midst.

The roar of the Lion of Judah is about to shatter the world system. It will bring down every stronghold illegitimately built by the rulers of darkness. With a mighty shout, the Lord of Lords and the King of Kings will prevail over His enemies! The Voice – God's Church shall be heard. But it all starts with us! If we are to be instruments through which God can speak – His Voice - we must familiarise ourselves with the way He communicates. Again, this requires study of His word and dedication to service in His kingdom. To be a "voice", we must know The Voice. The one who spoke everything into existence and who today upholds all things by the word of His power (Hebrews 1:3). In this regard, the single revelation we must walk in is this... *"God's word in my mouth, is as powerful as God's word in His own mouth!"* God is looking for a voice, will you be that voice?

Think of what Jeremiah accomplished after he became God's mouthpiece. He was called to uproot and tear down, to destroy and overthrow, to build and to plant (Jeremiah 1:9-10). That's a powerful calling. Through our obedience, we can do the same. We need the Lord to touch our lips and put His words in our mouths. So often, we can have negative words flowing from our lips rather than positive words that confess God's truth. Yet, God's Spirit wants to flow through us as rivers of living water (John 7:38). We must believe this, and in these challenging times we must learn to be His Voice and speak His truth!

Jeremiah 1:9-10,

> *"Then the Lord put forth His hand and touched my mouth, and the Lord said to me: "Behold, I have put My words in your mouth. See, I have this day set you over the nations and over*

the kingdoms, to root out and to pull down, to destroy and to throw down, to build and to plant."

What God declares in this passage of scripture should change your life! He says, *"I have put **My words in your mouth**."* God has put His words in your mouth! Incredible! Now, all He needs is a voice. So, don't get intimidated by the lies of the devil. You can be that voice! Jeremiah realized being one who speaks the word of God is an awesome task, so Jeremiah resisted and began to wrestle with God. He confessed how ill-equipped he was. Moses did the same thing! Yet, in spite of what he thought, Moses was used mightily by God. Moses was only armed with two things - a stutter and a stick. The stutter kept him humble, and the stick prepared him for the release of miraculous power. However, the key to his success was that he spoke (from his own mouth) the very words of God. He activated a creative force!

God's word never returns void. It will always accomplish that for which it has been sent. His word never fails!

The heavens may pass away and the mountains crumble, but His word will never pass away. His word is never wrong. So, when we stand with His words on our lips, when we speak His words through our mouths - with our voices - then that which His word declares will manifest.

Isaiah 40:3 refers to John the Baptist. He was the *"voice calling in the wilderness."* This is made clear by Matthew who interprets the verse for us (Matthew 3:1-3), and the same clarification is given by the writers of the other Gospel accounts (Mark 1:2-4, Luke 3:2-6, John 1:19-23). The story of John the Baptist should be of great encouragement to us. He was, quite literally, a voice crying in the wilderness - since he heralded the coming of the Christ in the wilderness of Judea (Matthew 3:1). He was the solitary "voice" that paved the way for the ministry of Jesus. How awesome is that!

The Holy Spirit wants to stir up the spirit of John the Baptist in our churches. We need more voices crying out in the wilderness today! Why not allow the Holy Spirit to bring out the *gift* that is within you?

Why not allow Him to put God's words in your mouth? Why not let Him breathe life into His words - as you boldly declare them?

Why not be the Voice of God?

15

Conclusion

The primary purpose for which all of the Gifts of the Holy Spirit are given is to build up the Church. Throughout the New Testament, we are reminded of this. However, there are two errors that are frequently made in today's churches.

The first is, to limit the scope of the *gifts* by embracing an overtly narrow view of what it means to "edify" the church body. The modern church outlook is inclined to focus on activities that contribute, in some immediate and fairly obvious way, to a statistical measure of effectiveness. It is what's commonly referred to as the "numbers game," and it's very prevalent in the entertainment industry. However, it is not meant to be practiced in the church. After all, pastors, evangelists and worship leaders, etc., are not called to be superstars, or reach celebrity status. Building (*edifying*) the church, therefore, should not be based on the number of conversions/decisions made, baptisms, attendance, membership figures, or offerings. While it may encourage Christians to know what has been achieved in these areas, for anything to be truly "edifying", the Gifts the Holy Spirit must be conspicuous – together with the presence of God and the anointing on His word.

As mentioned previously, the Holy Spirit and His Gifts serve to *magnify* the presence of God in the church, and this in itself is edifying. Indeed, when God's Spirit inspired the Scriptures, He placed no limitation or quota on His workings or *gifts*. In neither Romans 12 or 1 Corinthians 12 can we find a single reference to evaluating "edification" by numbers. There is no suggestion that we should be trying to measure the effectiveness of the Holy Spirit in any way whatsoever.

Measuring effectiveness by using church statistics arises from a desire to be popular and accepted. This is dangerous and not scriptural. God's Word repeatedly emphasises the need for us to surrender and be obedient, and to create an environment where the *gifts* can be exercised to their full measure. Our duty is to yield, and the Holy Spirit's duty is to produce the results. If they were *gifts* of the Church, then every local church would be responsible for producing results and would also be required to deliver numbers and statistics, etc. However, that is not the case! These are Gifts of the Holy Spirit, therefore, we should steer away from the numbers game. God alone knows how to build His Church.

The second common error, practiced in churches today, is the restrictions placed on the operations of the *gifts*. This is regularly implemented so that the *gifts* conform to our formal church programs or corporate worship events. Yet, there is no indication, anywhere in Scripture, that we are to limit the employment of *spiritual gifts*. The Holy Spirit was not sent to take part in organized programs that merely benefit the leadership of a local congregation. I Corinthians 14 provides guidelines for some of the Gifts of the Holy Spirit. These include; *prophecy, tongues, interpretation of tongues* and *teaching*. However, nothing in this chapter mentions that the aforementioned *spiritual gifts* are to be exercised exclusively during organized corporate events.

In fact, many New Testament examples indicate that the *gifts* were frequently exercised outside of church. The Book of Acts is full of spontaneous street ministry. In Acts 9, Ananias acted on a prophecy he had received in his own home and went to the house of an antagonist, the cruel Saul of Tarsus, to lay hands on him. Also, at the end of Acts 8, Philip explained the meaning of a passage about Jesus to an Ethiopian eunuch while riding in his chariot. What's more, Paul is said to have taught in numerous places, including the School of Tyrranus and several private homes, which then became meeting places for the early church. Finally, in Acts 27, while being held captive, Paul prophesied on three separate occasions to the centurion guarding him and to the master of the ship in which they were sailing.

As for those *gifts* not mentioned in I Corinthians 14, it should be noted that they were still seen, in the Book of Acts, to manifest predominantly outside of any organized corporate worship. For example, only one of the many healings mentioned occurred during a worship service, and even that one occurred during a service simply because someone died while Paul was preaching (Acts 20:9-10). Likewise, when the Holy Spirit came on the Day of Pentecost, He quickly moved out of the house into the street where the *signs* could be observed by thousands of people (Acts 2:1-6; 41). Furthermore, there is nothing that would logically limit the employment of any spiritual gift as the *gifts* were always intended to manifest "when the need arises." Wherever *edification* is necessary, in or out of the church, that's where we will find the Holy Spirit and His *gifts*.

Therefore, we must be careful not to end up in a ditch on either side of the road. We cannot in any way restrict or limit the multifaceted operations of the Holy Spirit and His Gifts.

That means, we cannot measure the effectiveness of the Spirit's ministry by numbers or popularity. He is not looking for flattery or self-promotion. He is God! Likewise, we cannot restrict the Holy Spirit to functioning within our organised corporate events, and nothing else. As mentioned, in the previous chapter, the *gifts* are absolutely necessary if we are to increase the presence of God in our services. However, we must also understand that God's presence goes with us everywhere, and consequently, we should have a balanced view when dealing with spiritual matters.

What brings most glory to God is having the *gifts* operating effectively in every service, together with the *gifts* operating efficiently in our personal lives. Whenever I give examples of the *gifts* having manifest in my life, I always explain the "tri-activity" that I have experienced (in the home, ministry and in business). My genuine expectation (unceasingly) has been for the gifts to manifest *wherever* and *whenever* there is a need! In this regard, the Holy Spirit has been faithful to guide and inspired me.

Being *"led by the Holy Spirit,"* results in the most exciting life you can ever imagine. Every day can be a thrilling adventure for those of us who know the reality of being "led" by the Holy Spirit and living continuously, moment by moment, under His gracious direction. Nonetheless, if we are going to be used to effectively engage in the operation of the *gifts*, we must first learn how to be *"led by the Spirit."* Paul writes, *"For all who are **led** by the Spirit of God these are sons of God"* (Romans 8:14). We will find several passages that refer to the Holy Spirit witnessing directly to our spirit (Romans 8:15-17; 8:26-27; 9:1). Hence, we should acknowledge that the Holy Spirit intends to direct our lives in more specific ways, and that this is all a part of what it means to be *"led by the Spirit."*

It should also be noted that the apostle Paul says **all** of God's children are *"led by the Spirit"*, not just some of them. Since we are children of God, we should therefore be safe and secure in Him - even when we are not as responsive or obedient to His leading as we ought to be. Kenneth Berding says,

> *"Attentiveness to the written Word sensitises us to the ways of the Spirit, to His priorities, and to His patterns... then when the time comes, despite all the noise in our lives, we become accustomed to distinguishing the Spirit from other voices whenever the Spirit chooses to lead us in this manner"*

Probably the most important thing we can do to develop sensitivity to the Holy Spirit's guidance (in addition to saturating ourselves in the Word), is to spend a significant amount of time praying in the Spirit. That way, we can be led in any direction! For me, it's been a matter of *"believing in divine appointments."* I have taught myself to see the hand of God orchestrating and supervising the countless events and divine appointments that invade my life. I have familiarised myself enough to be able to differentiate His voice from all the other voices that surround me. Every time I respond to the Spirit's promptings, I receive confirmation that He is in fact the Spirit of God and no other spirit. Subsequently, I have become progressively able to discern what the Spirit is doing and what's directly expected of me.

With that said, as children of God, we can all be confident that it's God who leads us into the various assignments He places in our path each day. Yes, we can be self-assured that He has already prepared them as a means of blessing those we come into contact with. Knowing this, it should cause us to pray, *"God use me in the lives of others, and let your Spirit manifest His gifts today in greater measure than ever before."*

We must truly appreciate the reality that God does in fact want to use us and that He has more faith in us than we have in ourselves. This is why He has entrusted us with the marvellous Gifts of the Holy Spirit. Right now, each of us ought to be expectant, confident, and full of faith! The Church needs to be *built up,* and each day we have the opportunity to join the Master Builder in performing this divine work. A supernatural work that can transform lives and change a nation! Therefore, I encourage you to study the *gifts,* acquire knowledge (through God's word) concerning spiritual matters, and then become sensitive to the Holy Spirit's leading. You will be amazed at what God can do through you!